THE CATHOLIC UNIVERSITY OF AMERICA
CANON LAW STUDIES
No. 168

APOSTATES AND FUGITIVES FROM RELIGIOUS INSTITUTES

AN HISTORICAL CONSPECTUS AND COMMENTARY

BY THE

REV. ALBERT JOSEPH RIESNER, C.SS.R., J.C.L.
Priest of the Baltimore Province

A DISSERTATION

Submitted to the Faculty of Canon Law of the Catholic University of America in Partial Fulfillment of the Requirements for the Degree of Doctor of Canon Law

THE CATHOLIC UNIVERSITY OF AMERICA PRESS
WASHINGTON, D. C.
1942

Imprimi Potest:

GULIELMUS T. MCCARTY, C.SS.R.,

Superior Provincialis.

Brooklynii, die 4 maii, 1942.

Nihil Obstat:

HIERONYMUS D. HANNAN, A.M., LL.B., S.T.D., J.C.D.,

Censor Deputatus.

Washingtonii, die 15 maii, 1942.

Imprimatur:

✠ MICHAEL J. CURLEY, D.D.,

Archiepiscopus Baltimoriensis-Washingtoniensis.

Baltimorae, die 15 maii, 1942.

Printed by

THE PAULIST PRESS

New York, N. Y.

51

TO

OUR MOTHER OF PERPETUAL HELP

AND

ST. ALPHONSUS DE LIGUORI

DOCTOR OF BOTH LAWS

DOCTOR OF THE CHURCH

TABLE OF CONTENTS

FOREWORD

MAN has a strong attachment to the material things of this world, to the pleasures of sense, and to his own will. Religious try to keep these attachments in check by the vows of poverty, chastity and obedience in the religious state. It should be no cause of surprise to find at times, religious who, drawn by these attachments, despise the grace of God, and on their own authority desert the religious institute in which they are professed. But the defection of these few does not derogate from the excellence of the state itself. On the contrary it sets in bolder relief the fidelity of those who persevere in fulfilling their sacred pledges to Almighty God.

This dissertation is not an exhaustive study of the history of the law on the unlawful departure from a religious institute, but rather a conspectus of the development of the law as found in the sources available to the writer.

The religious who deserts his institute with the intention of not returning is an apostate; he who deserts it temporarily is a fugitive. The purpose of this dissertation is to determine the extension of the terms "apostate" and "fugitive," the penalties incurred by apostates and fugitives, their obligations, the obligations of their superiors and the dispositions of law relative to the temporal goods acquired and used by them.

Apostates and fugitives may commit the qualified crimes which are punished with automatic dismissal. In as far as they are apostates and fugitives they are subject to the legislation described in this dissertation, but their qualified crimes are not within its scope.

The writer takes this occasion to express his gratitude to the Congregation of the Most Holy Redeemer, and especially to the Very Rev. William T. McCarty, C.SS.R., the Provincial of the Baltimore Province, for the privilege of advanced studies in Canon Law, to the Faculty of Canon Law of the Catholic University of America for their helpful assistance, to his sister who typed his manuscript, and to all who in any way aided in the preparation of this dissertation.

CHAPTER I

THE DESERTION OF THE RELIGIOUS STATE

"STATE" in its widest sense is, according to St. Thomas, a certain differentiation of position of an object corresponding to its characteristic nature, by which the object becomes, as it were, fixed and immobilized.[1] Specifically a state of life may be defined as a stabilized manner of living, or a fixed condition of life, arising from a permanent and not easily changeable cause. It connotes a complexus of acts, duties, occupations and manner of acting, the constant performance of which gives to a person's life not only its material nature, but also its specific character.[2] The chief element of a state is its stability or permanence.[3] This permanence must be caused by something which is extrinsic to the person in the state, and renders difficult any desertion of the state.[4] The state of a person is the external juridic condition of that person. It gives rise to rights and obligations, as determined by the society which wields authority over that state.[5]

The states of life concerned with the spiritual end of men are necessarily subject to the authority of the Church. By divine institution there are in the church clerics and laity: both can be religious.[6] By reason of the perfection of their state, the faithful may be classified among those who are in the state of the common Christian life, *viz.*, priests, inferior clerics and ordinary Christians, and those who are in the state of perfection, *viz.*, bishops and religious.[7] The epis-

[1] S. Thomas Aquinas, *Opera Omnia* (24 tomes in 15, Parmae, 1852-1869), Tom. III, *Summa Theologica*, IIa, IIae, q. 183, a. 1 (hereafter to be cited as *Summa Theologica*).

[2] Larraona, "Commentarium Codicis,"—*Commentarium pro Religiosis et Missionariis*, II (1921), 134-139 (hereafter to be cited as *CpR*).

[3] *Summa Theologica, loc. cit.*

[4] Bouix, *Tractatus de Jure Regularium* (2 vols., Parisiis, 1857), I, 4.

[5] Chelodi, *Ius de Personis* (Tridenti: Libr. Edit. Tridentum, 1922), n. 243; Goyeneche, "De Transitu ad aliam Religionem,"—*CpR*, I (1920), 21-30.

[6] Canon 107; Champoux, "The Clerical and Lay State Versus the Religious State,"—*The Jurist*, I (1941), 135-138.

[7] *Summa Theologica*, IIa, IIae, q. 184, aa. 5, 6.

copacy is a state of the exercise of perfection. The religious life is a state of the acquisition of perfection.[8] Religious profess the same moral and ascetic doctrine as other Christians, observe the same precepts, but take the three vows in the common life according to the evangelical counsels in order that they may the more easily attain Christian perfection.[9]

Catholic scholars [10] maintain that the religious state, namely, the permanent and abiding profession of the evangelical counsels, was immediately and substantially instituted by Christ.[11] From apostolic times men and women have heeded the call of Christ to the perfection of the Christian life,[12] the first of whom were *virgins* and *ascetics*.[13] But it cannot be proved that in these early years of the Church there existed a complete and perfect religious state in which the three essential vows were taken.[14]

[8] Suarez, *Opera Omnia* (26 tomes, Parisiis, 1856-1861), Tr. VII, lib. I, c. XV, and lib. II, c. I (hereafter to be cited as Suarez); Bouix, *op. cit.*, I, 18-20.

[9] Suarez, Tr. VII, lib. I, c. X; *Summa Theologica,* IIa, IIae, q. 184, a. 3; Schwientek, "Elementa status religiosi in S. Scriptura et in prima traditione ecclesiastica,"—*CpR,* I (1920), 315.

[10] Suarez, Tr. VIII, lib. III, c. II, nn. 3, 8; Heimbucher, *Die Orden und Kongregationen der katholischen Kirche* (3. ed., 2 vols., Paderborn: Schöningh, 1933-1934), I, 410, n. 10; Piatus Montensis, *Praelectiones Iuris Regularis* (3. ed., 2 vols., Tornaci, 1908). I, q. 26; Wernz, *Ius Decretalium ad usum Praelectionum in Scholis Textus Iuris Canonici, sive Iuris Decretalium* (2. ed., 6 vols., Romae: Typographia Polyglotta S. C. de Prop. Fide, 1908), Tom. III, pars II, n. 599 (hereafter to be cited as Wernz, *Ius Decretalium*); Coronata, *Institutiones Iuris Canonici* (5 vols., Taurini: Marietti, Vols. I and II, 2. ed., 1939, vols. III, IV, and V, 1. ed., 1933-1936), n. 502 (hereafter to be cited as Coronata, *Institutiones*).

[11] Cf. Matt., XVI, 24 (obedience); XIX, 12 (chastity); XIX, 21 (poverty).

[12] Steiger, "De propagatione et diffusione vitae religiosae,"—*Periodica de Re Canonica et Morali utili praesertim Religiosis et Missionariis,* XIII (1924), (36). Hereafter to be cited as *Periodica.*

[13] Steiger, *ibid.,* p. (37); Montalembert, *The Monks of the West* (2 vols., Boston, 1872), I, 171.

[14] Wernz, *Ius Decretalium,* Tom. III, pars II, n. 601. The outstanding element of the religious state, the common life, as found in the definition of the religious state in canon 487, is of ecclesiastical origin and does not pertain to the essence of the religious state. Cf. Suarez, Tr. VII, lib. II, c. IV, n. 4; Larraona, "Commentarium Codicis,"—*CpR,* II (1921), 134-139.

Though Christ substantially instituted the religious state, as a juridical institute it is of ecclesiastical origin and subject to the laws of the Church.[15] Canon 487 defines the religious state as "the firmly established manner of living in community, by which the faithful undertake to observe, not only the ordinary precepts, but also the evangelical counsels by means of the vows of obedience, chastity and poverty."[16] Canon 488, n. 1, defines a religious institute as a "society, approved by legitimate ecclesiastical authority, the members of which tend to evangelical perfection, according to the laws proper to their society, by the profession of public vows, whether perpetual or temporary, the latter renewable after the lapse of a fixed time"; and canon 488, n. 7, defines religious as "all those who have made profession of vows in any institute."[17]

The chief element of the religious state, as of all states, is stability or permanence. In the religious state stability in the observance of the evangelical counsels must be secured by a bond which induces an obligation of observing them.[18] This bond which is extrinsic to the person who is in the religious state, but is intrinsic to the state itself,[19] is the profession of public vows of obedience, chastity and poverty that are at least virtually perpetual.[20]

Since by their profession religious acquire a most firm and abiding state, in which they have a grave obligation to persevere, it is therefore a grave sin if they on their own authority dismiss the obligations they have taken upon themselves.[21] The vows, with which they have sealed their stability in the religious state, induce an

[15] Goyeneche, "De Transitu ad aliam Religionem,"—*CpR,* I (1920), 107-112.

[16] *Canonical Legislation Concerning Religious,* Authorized English Translation (Rome, Vatican Printing Office, 1919).

[17] Authorized English Translation.

[18] Suarez, Tr. VII, lib. II, c. III, n. 4; Prümmer, *Manuale Iuris Canonici* (5. ed., Friburgi Brisgoviae: Herder, 1927), q. 170.

[19] Wernz, *Ius Decretalium,* Tom. III, pars II, n. 590.

[20] Suarez, Tr. VII, lib. II, c. III, n. 5; Chelodi, *Ius de Personis,* n. 243.

[21] Wernz-Vidal, *Ius Canonicum ad Codicis normam exactum* (7 vols. in 8, Romae: Apud Aedes Universitatis Gregorianae, 1923-1938), Tom. III, n. 430.

obligation of divine law.[22] To desert the religious state on one's own authority, therefore, involves a grave offense against the virtue of religion.[23]

The act of religious profession comprises a twofold act on the part of the one taking the vows, first the taking of the vows, and secondly the *traditio* or surrendering of oneself to the institute accepting the vows.[24] The unlawful desertion of the religious state therefore involves a grave injustice, not only to God because of the vows, but also to the institute because of this surrender of oneself to the institute. It deprives God and the institute of what is due to them.[25]

Moreover, since in the present law the common life is an integral part of the religious state,[26] religious who unlawfully desert the state commit a grave offense against this ecclesiastical law.

Etymologically the word "apostasy" comes from the Greek. It is composed of the preposition ἀπό *off* and the noun στάσις *stand,* meaning the "desertion of the stand or manner of life that one has taken with the intention of perpetually adhering to it."[27]

St. Thomas says that apostasy denotes some desertion of or receding from God. Man is united to God in three ways, by faith, by subjection of the will to His precepts and by a special supererogatory way as in the religious or clerical state. By severing one of these unions with God one becomes an apostate. [28]

An apostate from the religious state is one who unlawfully de-

[22] *Summa Theologica,* IIa, IIae, q. 88, a. 10, ad 2; Suarez, Tr. VI, lib. IV, c. III, n. 1.

[23] Suarez, Tr. VIII, lib. III, c. I, nn. 2, 15; Lehmkuhl, *Theologia Moralis* (10. ed., 2 vols., Friburgi Brisgroviae, 1902), I, n. 536.

[24] Frey, *The Act of Religious Profession,* The Catholic University of America Canon Law Studies, n. 63 (Washington, D. C.: The Catholic University of America, 1931), p. 6; Papi, *Religious in Church Law* (New York: Kenedy, 1924), p. 268.

[25] Suarez, Tr. VIII, lib. III, c. I, nn. 2, 15.

[26] Canons 487; 594, § 1.

[27] Benedictus XIV, *De Synodo Dioecesana* (4 vols., Lovanii, 1763), Lib. XIII, c. XL, n. 9.

[28] *Summa Theologica,* IIa, IIae, q. 12, a. 1.

parts from that state with the intention of not returning to it.[29] A fugitive is one who unlawfully departs from the religious state but with the intention of returning to it.[30] Both the apostate and the fugitive desert the state they have professed,[31] the difference between them consisting in the fact that the apostate intends his departure to be perpetual whereas the fugitive intends his departure to be temporary.[32]

Suarez lists five ways in which a monastery is left unlawfully. The first way, he says, is that of leaving for a short time without permission, but with no intention of deserting the religious state. This does not constitute apostasy or flight. He then distinguishes between apostates and fugitives and between those who when leaving wear the habit or who put off the habit.[33] Since the habit is not essential to the religious state, but is an accidental sign of one's profession, the wearing or doffing of the habit would not change the status of the apostate or fugitive under the present law.

The Church approves of another state in which those who belong to it imitate religious state by living in common under the government of superiors, but do not seal their stability in their state by the profession of public vows of obedience, chastity and poverty, which are essential to the religious state. Those who are in this state are called members of societies whose members live in common without vows. The members seal their stability in the state by private vows, by an oath or by promises.[34] All these have an obligation by divine law to persevere in their state, those who take vows or an oath by the virtue of religion, those who make promises by the virtue of

[29] Ferraris, *Prompta Bibliotheca Canonica, Juridica, Moralis, Theologica, necnon Ascetica, Polemica, Rubristica, Historica* (8 vols., Parisiis, 1860-1863), s. v. "Apostasia," n. 21.

[30] Ferraris, *ibid.*, n. 25.

[31] A religious does not enter the religious state *in abstracto* but as a member of a particular institute. Consequently, a religious who deserts his institute also deserts the religious state and vice versa. Cf. *infra*, p. 66.

[32] Suarez, Tr. VIII, lib. III, c. I, nn. 2, 15; cf. *infra*, p. 62.

[33] Tr. VIII, lib. III, c. I.

[34] In this dissertation the expression "societies whose members live in common without vows" will be used for all such societies, irrespective of the fact that the members of some of these societies take private vows.

fidelity.[35] All have an obligation to persevere by ecclesiastical law, since they are bound by their respective constitutions which are ecclesiastical law, and also are bound by most of the obligations of religious, which they cannot observe outside their state. As will be proved later, members of societies living in common without vows cannot be apostates in the strict sense, but they can be fugitives.[36]

[35] Suarez, Tr. V, lib. II, c. II, n. 3; Tr. VI, lib. IV, c. III, n. 1.
[36] *Infra*, pp. 54, 55, 71.

Part I

Historical Conspectus

CHAPTER II

FROM THE BEGINNING TO GREGORY I
(c. 325-590)

Article 1. The Canonical Legislation

The first canonical legislation against monks who illicitly left their monastery with the intention to desert their monastic state appears to be contained in the *"Decrees and Constitutions for Monks and Anchorites"* found appended to the Ecumenical Council of Nicaea held in the year 325. However, these "Decrees and Constitutions" are certainly unauthentic and of a later date.[1]

Chapter 14 of these "Decrees and Constitutions" stated that if a monk, despising his profession, left the monastery and went to any city or village to live as a layman, he could not continue to wear the monastic habit, since such action brought contempt on his fellow-monks and created a bad name for monks in general.[2]

Though the period after the Council of Nicaea saw the spread of monasticism in the East through the efforts of SS. Athanasius (c. 297-373), Basil (329-379) and John Chrysostom (c. 344-407) and in the West through the efforts of SS. Jerome (c. 342-420), Augustine (354-430), Hilary of Poitiers (c. 315-367) and Martin of Tours (c. 316-397), the legislation tending to prevent the vagrancy of monks was meager.

[1] Hefele-Leclercq, *Histoire des Conciles* (10 vols. in 19, Paris: Letouzey et Ané, 1907-1938), Tom. I, pars I, p. 515.

[2] Mansi, *Sacrorum Conciliorum Nova et Amplissima Collectio* (53 vols. in 59, Parisiis, 1901-1927), II, 1018 (hereafter to be cited as Mansi).

A council held at Hippo (393) [3] and the III Council of Carthage (c. 397) [4] ordained that consecrated virgins when deprived of their parents were to be commended to the care of the bishops or of a priest, in a monastery of virgins or with some reputable women, lest they become vagrants and injure the reputation of the Church.

Pope Innocent I (402-417) in a letter to Victricius, Bishop of Rouen, said that monks who, after having lived for a while in a monastery, were advanced to the clerical orders were not to depart from their first purpose and resolve.[5]

The II Council of Arles (443) stated that those who after the profession of the religious life had apostatized and returned to the world and did not seek penance were not to be admitted to the communion of the faithful, nor were they to be admitted to the clerical office. After they had done penance they were not allowed to put on the secular dress under penalty of "alienation" from the Church.[6]

A synod held in Ireland (c. 450) under the presidency of St. Patrick stated that a monk who went into another parish without letters from his abbot was not to be given any food and was to be punished by his abbot as a wanderer.[7]

[3] C. 9—Mansi, III, 850.

[4] C. 9—Mansi, III, 885; Schroeder, *Disciplinary Decrees of the General Councils* (St. Louis, London: Herder, 1937), p. 22, footnote.

[5] C. 3, C. XVI, q. 1; Mansi, III, 1035; Migne, *Patrologiae Cursus Completus, Series Latina* (221 vols., Parisiis, 1844-1864), XX, 477 (hereafter to be cited as *MPL*); Jaffé, *Regesta Pontificum Romanorum* (2. ed., 2 tom. in 1 vol., correctam et auctam auspiciis Gulielmi Wattenbach curaverant S. Loewenfeld, F. Kaltenbrunner, P. Ewald, Lipsiae, 1885-1888), n. 286. Hereafter the letters L, K and E will be joined with the letter J in designation of the editor of the document cited from Jaffé's work in its second edition. The letter of Innocent I stands designated thus: J K, n. 286.

[6] C. 25—c. 69, D. L.; Mansi, VII, 881. Various expressions were used to express the penalty of excommunication. Cf. Hyland, *Excommunication, Its Nature, Historical Development and Effects,* The Catholic University of America Canon Law Studies, n. 49 (Washington, D. C.: The Catholic University of America, 1928), p. 18.

[7] C. 34—Mansi, VI, 520. This synod is of doubtful authenticity—McNeill, and Gamer, *Medieval Handbooks of Penance* (New York: Columbia University Press, 1938), pp. 75-78.

The first general legislation against apostate and vagrant or fugitive monks is found in the IV Ecumenical Council, held at Chalcedon in 451. At that time there was a large number of monks who wandered from place to place, casting off discipline and bringing discredit on their state.[8] There was also a host of Eastern monks, more zealous than orthodox, who interfered in civil and ecclesiastical matters, appearing even at this Council.[9] To check these disorders, the Council at the proposal of the Emperor Marcian (450-457), in canon 4 decreed that all monks should remain in the place where they had renounced the world and should not leave it to burden themselves with ecclesiastical or secular matters unless they were commanded to do so by the bishop.[10] Canon 23 of the same Council went further and stated that those monks who had not been sent by their bishops on business, but on the contrary had perhaps even been excommunicated by him, and were disturbing ecclesiastical affairs in the city of Constantinople and corrupting homes, were to be warned to leave the city; and if they refused they were to be put out and compelled, by the "defender" of the Church of Constantinople, to return to their monasteries.[11]

With regard to apostate monks who had given up their monastic state for secular honors or for entry into the miiltary service, canon 7 of the Council stated that if they did not repent and return to their monasteries they were to be excommunicated.[12]

Pope Leo I (440-461), in writing to Rusticus, Bishop of Narbonne, said that once one had taken the resolve of being a monk he could not at will give it up without committing sin, for what one had vowed to God, he had to fulfill.[13] Hence he who had left his profession as a monk to enter marriage or the military service, was to be cleansed by public penance, for although military service was

[8] Montalembert, *op. cit.*, I, 218, 262.

[9] Montalembert, *loc. cit.*; Schroeder, *op. cit.*, p. 92.

[10] C. 12, C. XVI, q. 1; Mansi, VII, 353, Schroeder, *op. cit.*, p. 92.

[11] C. 17, C. XVI, q. 1; Mansi, VII, 367; Schroeder, *op. cit.*, p. 121.

[12] C. 3, C. XX, q. 3; Mansi, VII, 362; Schroeder, *op. cit.*, p. 96.

[13] Deut. xxiii, 21; Ps. xlix, 44.

in itself innocent and marriage honorable, yet the deserting of a better choice was a transgression.[14]

The period from the Council of Chalcedon to the time of Pope Gregory the Great (590) saw the break-up of the Roman Empire, the invasion of the barbarians, the advent of St. Benedict and the spread of monasticism in Gaul.[15] During this period of decentralization very little legislation emanated from the Roman See. The numerous local, provincial and national councils, especially those of Gaul, continued the effort to stop monks from wandering about except for reasons of necessary business and with the written permission of their superiors,[16] stating that vagrant monks were to be kept in custody by the bishop and recalled to the monastery by their abbots.[17] If they did not heed the verbal warning they were to be coerced by more severe methods and were even to be excommunicated.[18] Vagrant monks could not be ordained clerics in any city or parish without the testimonials of their abbots.[19] Abbots, if they wandered from their monastery without permission, were to be corrected by the bishops.[20]

The Council of Chalcedon (451) had forbidden monks under threat of excommunication to give up their monastic state and to return to the secular life.[21] The particular councils extended this threat to sacred virgins who relinquished their chosen state.[22]

[14] C. 1, C. XX, q. 3; Mansi, VI, 405; *MPL*, LV, 1207; *Bullarum, Diplomatum et Privilegiorum Sanctorum Romanorum Pontificum Tauriensis Editio* (24 tomes in 25 vols., Augustae Taurinorum, 1857-1872), I, 42 (hereafter to be cited as *Bull. Rom. Taur.;* J K, n. 544.

[15] Butler, *Benedictine Monachism* (London, New York: Longmans, Green & Co., 1919), pp. 1-10; Montalembert, *op. cit.*, I, 266-294, 305-315, 449-451.

[16] Council of Angers (453), c. 6—Mansi, VII, 901; Council of Vannes (465), c. 6—Mansi, VII, 953.

[17] Council of Agde (506), c. 27—Mansi, VIII, 329; I Council of Orleans (511), c. 19—Mansi, VIII, 354.

[18] Council of Agde (506), c. 38—Mansi, VIII, 331.

[19] Council of Agde (506), c. 27—Mansi, VIII, 329.

[20] V Council of Paris (554), c. 3—Mansi, IX, 702.

[21] C. 7—c. 3, C. XX, q. 3; Mansi, VII, 362; Schroeder, *op. cit.*, p. 96.

[22] Council of Tours (461), c. 6—Mansi, VII, 946; III Council of Lyons (582), c. 3—Mansi, VIII, 942.

Article II. The Monastic Rules

Though the monastic rules were not ecclesiastical laws yet they are indicative of the obligations which the monks took upon themselves by their monastic profession. Following the words of Deuteronomy: "That which is once gone out of thy lips, thou shalt observe, and shalt do as thou hast promised to the Lord thy God," [23] from the very beginning the monastic founders stressed the permanence of the state once one had entered upon it.

The Abbot Isaias who was a contemporary of St. Anthony (250-356) said in his "Rule for Monks": "Dearly beloved brother, if you have left the world and have given yourself to God, do penance for your sins and keep the course of life that you have embraced." [24]

Among the "Precepts and Judgments" of St. Pachomius (292-346) is found one which said that "if one promises to observe the rules of the monastery, begins to do so and then gives them up, when he comes back to do penance, claiming that because of weakness of the body he could not keep them, he shall be made to live with the sick and eat with the lazy until he performs the acts of penance which he promised." [25]

St. Basil (329-379) in his *Regulae Fusius Tractatae* said: "One who had dedicated himself to God and then goes over to another kind of life, becomes a sacrilegious thief in taking back a gift consecrated to God. To such it is fitting that the doors of the confrères should no longer be opened." [26] In his "Monastic Constitutions" he said that his monks were not to leave the monastery or have any possessions,[27] and that deserters were to be warned and brought back to the place they had left, but if they would not obey they were to be avoided and thus forced to return to the sheepfold.[28]

St. Benedict (480-543) wrote the first rule for the monks of the West. In Chapter 58, "On the manner of reception of the brethren,"

[23] Deut. xxiii, 23.

[24] *MPL,* CIII, 427.

[25] Preceptum 171—*MPL,* XXIII, 83.

[26] Interrogatio 16—Migne, *Patrologiae Cursus Completus, Series Graeca* (161 vols., Parisiis, 1856-1866), XXXI, 950 (hereafter to be cited as *MPG*).

[27] C. 34—*MPG,* XXXI, 1423.

[28] C. 33—*MPG,* XXXI, 1422.

one reads that after a year of novitiate, during which the rule was read to the novices three times, the novice promised stability, the conversion of his ways and obedience, knowing that from that day he was not allowed to leave the monastery.[29] This stability which the monk promised had a double aspect. It included not only perseverance in the monastic state, but also perseverance until death in the monastery in which the monk was professed.[30]

In chapter 29, "On whether the brethren who leave the monastery must be taken back," one reads that if a monk left the monastery through his own fault, and wished to return, he first must promise to make amends for his fault, and then was to be assigned to the last place, that from this his humility might be proved. But if he left again he was to be received back even to the third time, knowing that after that the opportunity of returning was to be denied to him.[31]

In chapter 61, "On how peregrine monks are to be received," the abbot was warned not to receive a monk from another monastery, unless the monk had the permission and testimonial letters of his abbot.[32]

The rules of the monastic founders of Gaul during the sixth century also prohibited the abandoning of the religious state. St. Caesarius of Arles (470-542) in his "Rule for Monks,"[33] and in his "Rule for Virgins,"[34] likewise St. Aurelian, the immediate successor of St. Caesarius in the see of Arles, in his "Rule for Monks,"[35] and in his "Rule for Virgins,"[36] stated that monks and nuns should persevere until death in the monastery in which they were professed and should not presume, nor be permitted, to leave the monastery, on account of the saying of the prophet: "One thing I have asked of

[29] Butler, *Sancti Benedicti Regula Monasteriorum* (3. ed., Friburgi Brisgoviae: Herder, 1935), c. 58; *S. P. Benedicti Regula cum commentariis*, c. 58—*MPL*, LXVI, 803-806.

[30] Butler, *Benedictine Monachism*, pp. 123-134; *MPL*, LXVI, 821.

[31] Butler, *Sancti Benedicti Regula Monasteriorum*, c. 29; *MPL*, LXVI, 523.

[32] Butler, *Sancti Benedicti Regula Monasteriorum*, c. 61; *MPL*, LXVI, 853.

[33] C. 1—*MPL*, LXVII, 1099.

[34] C. 1—*MPL*, LXVII, 1107.

[35] C. 2—*MPL*, LXVIII, 389.

[36] C. 1—*MPL*, LXVIII, 399.

the Lord, that I may dwell in the house of the Lord all the days of my life." [37]

St. Ferreolus (+581), Bishop of Uzès (now Nîmes), in his "Rule for Monks" stated that if a monk presumed to leave his monastery without permission of the abbot, he should fast twice the number of days that he was out of the monastery, no wine should be given him on those days, and the abbot was to determine as to the sort of food. Moreover fugitives should be sought after.[38]

Article III. The Roman Law

In this period of union between Church and State laws were enacted by the Roman Emperors, chiefly by Justinian, against vagrant or fugitive and apostate monks. The earliest legislation on this matter was enacted shortly after the Council of Chalcedon (451). It endeavored to put a check on vagrancy of monks. Numerous monks wandered from town to town, casting aside discipline and bringing discredit on their state.[39] In an effort to combat this, Emperor Theodosius II and Valentinian III in 455 decreed that all members of the clergy and monks who would come to the City of Constantinople for the purpose of transacting ecclesiastical business, or on account of religion, should be furnished with letters from the bishop to whom they owed obedience. If they did not comply with this, they were to have themselves to blame if they were not considered as clerics or monks.[40]

The constitution of Emperors Leo I and Anthemius addressed to Zeno in the year 471 had the same purpose as canons 4 and 23 of the Council of Chalcedon.[41] This constitution forbade monks to leave their monasteries and to be engaged in various affairs in Antioch and other cities, except the *aprocrisiarii* who were allowed to

[37] Ps. xxvi, 4.

[38] C. 20—*MPL,* LXVI, 966.

[39] Montalembert, *The Monks of the West,* I, 218.

[40] C. (1. 3) 22. *Corpus Iuris Civilis,* 3 vols., Berolini, 1928-1929. *Institutiones,* quas recognovit P. Krueger; *Digesta,* quae recognovit T. Mommsen, et retractavit P. Krueger; *Codex Iustinianus,* quem recognovit et retractavit P. Krueger; *Novellae,* quas recognovit R. Schoell, et absolvit G. Kroll.

[41] *Supra,* p. 9.

go into the cities for necessary business. The *aprocrisiarii* were warned, when they went into the cities, not to take part in disputes about religious worship or dogma, nor by their counsels, which tended to sedition and tumult, to pervert the more simple minds of the people. Transgressors were subject to the severity of the law.[42]

Because of suspicion in the minds of some as to whether this legislation had been enacted, the Emperor Justinian in a constitution re-enacted it in more perfect form.[43] Justinian moreover ordered the local bishops to see that neither monks nor nuns wandered about through the cities. If they had any necessary answers to make in court they should make them through the *aprocrisiarii.*[44]

Justinian also sanctioned as laws the canons of the first four general councils.[45] Thus two canons of the Council of Chalcedon concerning vagrant monks obtained the force of civil law, canon 4 which prohibited monks from leaving their monastery and from burdening themselves with ecclesiastical and secular affairs,[46] and canon 23 which stated that monks who were in the City of Constantinople without the permission of their superiors and were disturbing ecclesiastical affairs and corrupting homes were to be warned to return to their monasteries if necessary under compulsion from the "defender" of the city.[47]

The first legislation in regard to apostate monks who deserted the religious state is found in the constitution of the Emperor Justinian cited above. He stated that in the future monks were not to be allowed to put off the religious habit and take up the sword or any kind of military service, or be invested in any dignity or be engaged in the courts, preferring human occupations to the service of God. Whoever did any of these forbidden things was to be handed over to the curia of the city from which he came and, if he was rich, was to be held to the performance of pecuniary duties

[42] C. (1. 3) 29.
[43] C. (1. 3) 52. 9.
[44] N. (123. 42).
[45] N. (131. 1).
[46] C. 12, C. XVI, q. 1; Mansi, VII, 359; Schroeder, *Disciplinary Decrees of the General Councils,* p. 92.
[47] C. 17, C. XVI, q. 1; Mansi, VII, 367; Schroeder, *op. cit.,* p. 121.

besides those in the curia.[48] This law was changed by Justinian in the Novels,[49] where he decreed that one who had left the monastery for the secular life was to be deprived of any dignity or military office by the bishop of the place and put into a monastery by the governor of the province, and if he had acquired any property after he left, the property belonged to the monastery in which he was placed. But if he apostatized a second time, then the governor of the province in which he was found was to retain him and make him an official of the curia subject to his authority.

Speaking of this attachment to the governor's service Justinian said that the result would be that he who despised the divine service would serve an earthly tribunal.[50] In this same novel Justinian warned such apostates that they would have to render an account to God for their action.[51] Moreover by virtue of the sanction given to the first four general councils,[52] the *anathema* (excommunication) of canon 7 of the Council of Chalcedon [53] against apostate monks who entered the military service or who attempted marriage received civil force. Slaves could become monks; but if a former slave deserted the monastery in which he had been professed, his former master could reclaim him.[54]

Roman law forbade not only the return to secular life, but also the transfer of a monk to another monastery. Anyone who had left his monastery to go to another was not to be received by the abbot, as such action showed inconstancy. Bishops and archimandrites were to prohibit this and thus preserve the gravity of the monastic state according to the sacred canons.[55]

In regard to the property which the apostate monk had brought to the monastery the law was always the same. They did not receive back the movable goods which they had brought with them,

[48] C. (1. 3) 52. 9 and 10.
[49] N. (123. 42).
[50] N. (5. 6).
[51] N. (5. 4).
[52] N. (131. 1).
[53] C. 3, C. XX, q. 3; Mansi, VII, 362; Schroeder, *op. cit.*, p. 96.
[54] N. (5. 2) 3.
[55] N. (5. 7).

even if no agreement was made as to them,[56] but these goods were to belong to the monastery from which they fled.[57] In the donation of immovable goods by monks the laws were to be observed whenever the right of revocation was not taken away from the monk.[58]

The law in regard to the property of those who transferred to another monastery was the same as for apostates, namely, it belonged to the monastery wherein they had renounced the world.[59]

[56] C. (1. 3) 38.
[57] C. (1. 3) 54. 7; N. (5. 4 and 6); N. (23. 37).
[58] C. (1. 3) 38.
[59] N. (123. 42); (5. 7).

CHAPTER III

GREGORY I TO THE DECREE OF GRATIAN (590-1140)

ARTICLE I. THE CANONICAL LEGISLATION

DURING this period many of the bishops were selected from the monasteries. In the year 590 Gregory a monk of the monastery of St. Andrew in Rome was chosen by unanimous consent as the first monk to rule the See of Peter. Forced to abandon the cloister which he loved and cherished, Gregory I (590-604) was ever solicitous for the monastic state. Many of his letters concern vagrant or apostate monks.

In one of his first letters as pope he wrote to an old friend and fellow monk, Venantius, who had abandoned the monastic state for the married, begging him to enter into himself and return to the monastery.[1] In a letter to the subdeacon Anthemius, Pope Gregory ordered that monks be not allowed to go from one monastery to another; and if they had done so they were to be forced to return to the monastery in which they had renounced the world.[2] He moreover commanded Anthemius to seek after those monks who had attempted marriage and to force them to return to the monastery.[3] Writing to Felix, the Bishop of Messina, and to Peter the subdeacon he commanded that all dispersed monks be gathered into the monastery of St. Theodore under the government of Bishop Paulinus.[4] He

[1] Ep. I, 33 (34)—Mansi, IX, 1033-1054; *MPL,* LXXVII, 486-489; *Monumenta Germaniae Historica, Epistolae,* Tom. I, pars I (ed. P. Ewald, Berolini, 1887), p. 45 (hereafter to be cited as *MGH*) ; J E, n. 1103.

[2] Ep. I, 40 (42)—c. 5, X, *de regularibus et transeuntibus ad religionem,* III, 31; Mansi, IX, 1058; *MPL,* LXXVII, 495; *MGH, Epistolae,* Tom. I, pars I, p. 55; J E, n. 1110.

[3] Ep. I, 40 (42)—c. 39, C. XXVII, q. 1; Mansi, *MPL, MGH,* and J E, *loc. cit.*

[4] Ep. I, 38 (40), 38 (41)—Mansi, IX, 1057, 1058; *MPL,* LXXVII, 493, 494; *MGH, Epistolae,* Tom. I, pars I, p. 51; J E, nn. 1108, 1109.

commanded Dominic, the Bishop of Carthage, to recall and teach obedience to those monks who had left the monastery because their abbot, Cumquodeus, had tried to enforce the regular discipline.[5]

Gregory was no less solicitous about nuns who of their own will returned to the world. They were to be sought after, recalled to their monastery and put under strict vigilance, but all with the greatest charity.[6] In another case he directed that a seduced nun be recalled and confined to her monastery.[7] Widows who, after they had taken the religious habit, sought the company of men and then apostatized, were to be excluded from the churches and the gatherings of the faithful, and put in prisons until they made satisfaction.[8]

Monasticism began in Spain during the fourth century, reached its perfection after the conversion of the Visigoths in 589, and began to decline by the time of the Arab conquest in 712.[9] The Church in Spain during the Visigothic period was one of the best organized sections of Christendom. Provincial and national councils were of frequent occurrence.

The legislation against apostate and fugitive monks is found chiefly in the IV (633),[10] VI (638) [11] and XIII (683) [12] Provincial Councils of Toledo. The canons of these councils stated that monks, widows and virgins were not allowed to leave the monastery to return to the word or to enter marriage. But if they did so they were to be recalled and forced to return to the same monastery and

[5] Ep. VII, 32 (35)—*MPL,* LXXVII, 895; *MGH, Epistolae,* Tom. I, pars I, p. 481; J E, n. 1478.

[6] Ep. VIII, 8, 9—c. 18, 19, C. XXVII, q. 1; *MPL,* LXXVII, 912, 913; *MGH, Epistolae,* Tom. II (ed. P. Ewald et L. Hartmann, Berolini, 1893-1899), pars I, pp. 10, 11; J E, n. 1495, 1496.

[7] Ep. X, 3 (8)—c. 15, C. XXVII, q. 1; *MPL,* LXXVII, 1071, 1072; *MGH, Epistolae,* Tom. II, pars II, p. 238; J E, n. 1770.

[8] C. 2, C. XXVII, q. 1.

[9] McKenna, *Paganism and Pagan Survivals in Spain up to the Fall of the Visigothic Kingdom,* The Catholic University of America Studies in Medieval History, New Series, Vol. I (Washington, D. C.: The Catholic University of America, 1938), pp. 145, 146.

[10] Cc. 49, 52, 53, 55—Mansi, X, 631, 632.

[11] C. 6—Mansi, X, 665.

[12] C. 11—Mansi, XI, 1073, 1074.

there do penance. If they preferred to remain deserters, they were to be excommunicated as apostates.

The XIII Council of Toledo (683) legislated against all those who received, advised, sheltered, showed kindness to, or in any way assisted apostate and vagrant monks. If one said that he thought he had taken in a simple cleric and did not know he was a deserter, his innocence was to be proved when, within eight days as required by law, he presented the deserter to the judge, and within the time stated in law returned him to the monastery from which he had fled. If the one who transgressed this law and who took in a deserter was a bishop, he, after having returned the monk and his property to the monastery, was excommunicated and was removed from office for a time equal to the time he had harbored the deserter. If the one who transgressed this law was a priest, deacon or religious, he was under the censure of penance for one year under the abbot of the deserter. Those whose predecessors in office had taken in or showed kindness to a deserter were not under the penalty if, within two months from the time of taking office, they made known the hiding place of the deserter and returned him to his monastery.[13]

During the seventh century the Lombards were in control of Italy. This weakened the power of the Papacy and hence very little legislation came from the Roman See. Gaul had been divided into kingdoms and there were continual struggles between the last of the Merovingian kings. Provincial councils were few. One Gallic council, the V of Paris (615),[14] and the Synod of Autun (670) [15] legislated against vagrant and apostate monks and nuns. At this time the local legislation of the churches of other regions was circulated through Gaul. Hence the law in regard to apostates and fugitives observed there was the same as elsewhere.[16]

[13] Capitulum 11—Mansi, XI, 1073, 1074.

[14] C. 12—Mansi, X, 542; *MGH, Legum Sect. III, Concilia,* 2 tomes and 1 supplement, Tom. I (ed. A. Maasson, Hannoverae, 1893), p. 189.

[15] C. 10—Mansi, XI, 124; *MGH, Legum Sect. III, Concilia,* Tom. I, p. 221.

[16] Van Hove, *Commentarium Lovaniense in Codicem Iuris Canonici,* Vol. I, Tom. I, (*Prolegomena*) (Mechliniae, Romae: Dessain, 1928), n. 133 (hereafter to be cited as *Prolegomena*).

The "Law of the Bavarians," issued during the period of the Merovingian kings in the Frankish Kingdom, stated that if one seduced a nun to leave her monastery and tried to marry her, the bishop with the aid of the duke was to seek her and return her to the monastery; and the seducer was to pay to her monastery double the usual fine for rape.[17]

During the last years of the Merovingian dynasty the king was the *de iure* ruler, but the *Major Domus* was the *de facto* ruler. In 747 Pepin became *Major Domus* and in 751 King of the Franks. At his time St. Boniface was laboring in the territory that is now Germany, but his influence was felt in the whole Frankish Kingdom.[18]

In the canonical instruction sent by Pope Zachary (741-752) to Pepin in the year 747, the pope spoke of the excommunication enacted in canon 7 of the Council of Chalcedon against apostate monks,[19] and also cited the letter of Pope Innocent I to Victricius,[20] which forbade monks who were clerics to abandon their first purpose and resolve, namely, the religious state.[21]

As Kings of the Franks Pepin and also his son, Charlemagne, dedicated themselves to political and ecclesiastical reform. Councils were again of frequent occurrence, and the canons of these councils had not only ecclesiastical but also civil force because of their repromulgation by the king. These councils restated the prohibition to leave one's monastery, imposing on the bishops the obligation to curb this abuse and to punish offenders with excommunication, and

[17] *Lex. Baiuvarionum*, Tit. I, cap. 11 (12)—Mansi, XVIIb, 100; *MGH, Legum Sect. I, Leges Nationum Germanicarum*, Tom. V, pars I (ed. E. von Schwind, Hannoverae, 1926), p. 283.

[18] Hughes, *A History of the Church* (2 vols., New York: Sheed & Ward, 1934-1935), II, 153, 154. The Frankish Kingdom at this time included what is present-day Germany and France, Italy being added later (c. 795).

[19] *Supra*, p. 9.

[20] *Supra*, p. 8.

[21] C. 9, 13—Mansi, XII, 330, 331; *MPL*, LXXXIX, 934; *MGH, Epistolae*, Tom. III, *Epistolae Merovingici et Karolini Aevi* (Berolini, 1892), Tom. I, p. 482, 483; J E, n. 2277.

even by putting them in solitary confinement until they came to their senses.[22]

In a council of the whole Frankish Church held in an unknown place in 745 under St. Boniface (c. 675-754) [23] it was enacted that monks were not allowed to go to Rome or wander about in any place unless they were acting under obedience of their abbot. But if a monastery fell into the hands of the laity, monks who wished to go to other monasteries were allowed to do so.[24]

Charlemagne (768-814) enacted laws in many Capitularies in regard to apostate and vagrant religious,[25] but they all repeated the canons of the Council of Chalcedon and previous local councils on this matter.

Louis the Pious (814-840) enacted legislation similar to that of has father Charlemagne.[26] In a "Decree for the restoration of the monastic life in the monastery of St. Dionysius" (832) it is related that certain monks who had abandoned the monastic life confessed

[22] Council of Mayence (813), cc. 12, 13, 22—*MGH, Legum Sect. III, Concilia,* Tom. II (ed. A. Werminghoff, Hannoverae et Lipsiae, 1906), pars I, pp. 264, 267; Mansi, XIV, 68, 71; VI Council of Paris (829), c. 28—*MGH, Legum Sect. III, Concilia,* Tom. II, pars II, p. 631; Mansi, XIV, 558; Council of Verneuil (844), c. 4—*MGH, Legum Sect. II, Capitularia Regum Francorum,* Tom. II (ed. V. Krause, Hannoverae, 1897), p. 384; Mansi, XIV, 382; II Council of Toul (860), c. 5—Mansi, XV, 560; Roman Synod (853), c. 28—Mansi, XIV, 1007.

[23] Kurth, *Saint Boniface,* Translated from the fourth French edition by Rt. Rev. Victor Day with insertions from the Latest Historical Findings by Rev. Francis Betten, E.J. (Milwaukee: Bruce, 1935), p. 86.

[24] C. 10—*MGH, Legum Sect. II, Capitularia,* Tom. I (ed. A. Boretius, Hannoverae, 1883), p. 35; Mansi, XII, 582, XVIIb, 172.

[25] *Capitulare Mantuanum II Generale* (c. 787), c. 2—*MGH, Legum Sect. II, Capitularia,* Tom. I, p. 196; *Capitulare Ecclesiasticum* (789), cc. 26, 40, 52 —*MGH, Legum Sect. II, Capitularia,* Tom. I, pp. 56, 57; *Capitulare Pippini Regis Italiae* (793), c. 2—Mansi, XVIIb, 535; *Capitulare Francofurtense* (794), c. 24—*MGH, Legum Sect. II, Capitularia,* Tom. I, p. 76; *Capitulare Missorum Generale* (802), c. 18—*MGH, Legum Sect. II, Capitularia,* Tom. I, p. 95; *Capitula De Examinandis Ecclesiasticis* (802), c. 17—*MGH, Legum Sect. II, Capitularia,* Tom. I, p. 111.

[26] *Capitulare Missorum* (814), c. 18—*MGH, Legum Sect. II, Capitularia,* Tom. I, p. 290; Mansi, XVIIb, 617.

their crime and renewed their profession in the same monastery before the gathering of the bishops.[27]

To this period also belong the spurious "Capitularies of Benedict the Levite." [28] In his first book the compiler forged two capitularies from Roman law sources.[29] He said that all the goods possessed by a monk who had left the monastery were to remain with the monastery. If the monk tried to go to another monastery he was not to be received.[30] If a monk had given up the monastic life he was to be attached by the governor of the province to the curia.[31] In his second book he repeated the capitulary concerning the property of monks who had left their monasteries,[32] and forged a capitulary from canon 25 of II Council of Arles (443),[33] which had stated that apostates were to be deprived of communion with the faithful, and not be admitted to the clerical office.[34] In his third book he forged a capitulary from canon 12 of the V Council of Paris (615).[35] This canon had stated that apostate monks and nuns who did not return to their monasteries when the bishop had warned them by letter were to be suspended from the reception of Communion for the rest of their life, and not be admitted to the Eucharist until they had returned and made satisfaction.[36]

St. Boniface (c. 675-754) had founded many monasteries in what is now Germany, especially the famous monastery of Fulda.[37] In an answer to the question proposed by St. Boniface, Pope Gregory

[27] Mansi, XVIIb, 675-680.

[28] Van Hove, *Prolegomena*, n. 160.

[29] They are taken from the *Summa de ordine ecclesiastico*, an epitome of the novels of Justinian.—Seckel, "Studien zu Benedictus Levita,"—*Neues Archiv der Gesellschaft für ältere deutsche Geschichtskunde*, XXXI (1905), 125, 126. This periodical hereafter to be cited as *NA*.

[30] Lib. I, c. 379—*MGH*, *Leges* (Hannover, 1837—Reprint 1925), Tom. II, Appendix, p. 68; Mansi, XVIIb, 905; cf. also N. (5. 4, 6, 7).

[31] Lib. I, c. 381—*MGH*, Mansi, *loc. cit.;* cf. also N. (123. 42).

[32] Lib. II, c. 108—*MGH*, *Leges*, Tom. II, appendix, p. 78; Mansi, XVIIb, 941.

[33] Seckel, "Studien zu Benedictus Levita,"—*NA*, XXXIV (1908), 372.

[34] C. 69, D. L; Mansi, VII, 881.

[35] Seckel, "Studien zu Benedictus Levita,"—*NA*, XL (1915), 100.

[36] Mansi, X, 542.

[37] Cf. Hughes, *A History of the Church*, II, 154.

II (715-731) said that those who in infancy had been put in a monastery by their parents were not allowed to leave even when they reached the age of puberty.[38] In the latter half of the next century two distinctively German [39] councils, the Council of Worms (868) [40] and the Council of Tribur (895),[41] stated that if those who had been put in a monastery as children presumed to leave they were to be forced to return.

The English councils of this period, like those on the continent, prohibited monks to go to another monastery without permission.[42] Vagrant monks could be received as guests only once.[43] Apostates as well as those who had been driven out of their monasteries were commanded to return to the monastery in which they had been professed. But if they had been taken into another monastery and then began to wander, they were obliged to return to the monastery in which they had been taken in.[44]

In the *Collectio Hibernensis* [45] is found a canon which said "that a monk should not be without government even for an hour." [46] In the "Excerpts of Egbert of York," which are prefixed to the penitential attributed to him,[47] monks were forbidden to wander from

[38] C. 2, C. XX, q. 1; *MPL,* LXXXIX, 526, n. 7; J E, n. 2174.

[39] About the year 870 Germany and France began to exist as separate kingdoms.—Hughes, *op. cit.*, p. 184.

[40] C. 22—Mansi, XV, 873.

[41] C. 27—c. 6, C. XX, q. 1; *MGH, Legum Sect. II, Capitularia,* Tom. II, p. 228. Mansi does not give the same reading of this canon as the sources cited. According to Mansi this Council applied canon 7 of the Council of Chalcedon only to apostates *ab ordine.*

[42] Council of Hereford (673), c. 4—Mansi, XI, 129; Constitutions of Odo, Archbishop of Canterbury (c. 943), c. 6—Mansi, XVIIa, 396.

[43] Council of Berghamsted (696), c. 8—Mansi, XII, 112.

[44] Council of Cloveshoe (747), c. 29—Mansi, XII, 407.

[45] Composed about the year 800.—Van Hove, *Prolegomena,* n. 132; McNeill-Gamer, *Medieval Handbooks of Penance,* p. 139.

[46] Lib. 38, c. 4—Mansi, XII, 133.

[47] McNeill-Gamer, *op. cit.*, p. 237; Albers, "Wann sind die Beda-Egbertschen Bussbücher verfasst worden, und wer ist ihr Verfasser,"—*Archiv für katholisches Kirchenrecht,* LXXXI (1901), 393-420.

their monastery and were obliged to remain in the monastic state whether their parents had put them in the monastery or whether they had entered of their own choice.[48]

The last part of the ninth and the early part of the tenth century offered no conciliar legislation on the matter here discussed. With the renaissance of Catholic life, due to the reform started by by the monastery of Cluny and the reform popes, councils were again held.[49]

The French and British Councils after the period of reform ordained that apostates from the religious life were to be excommunicated and forced to return to their monasteries.[50] This was a major excommunication and therefore those under it had to be avoided even in profane matters. This was strictly enforced in the Middle Ages.[51] Abbots and abbesses who refused to take back a repentant apostate were given three warnings and then suspended "from the community of the brethren" until they did so.[52] Meanwhile the repentant apostate was to live with clerics in some monastery or church.[53]

One papal letter of this period, that of Alexander II (1061-1073), forbade monks, according to the tenor of the Council of Chalcedon and the Rule of St. Benedict, to leave their monasteries and to go about towns and villages.[54]

Thus stood the law in regard to apostate and vagrant monks after nine centuries of monastic life, as we find it in the "Decree of

[48] Num. 65, 66, 93—Mansi, XII, 419, 421.

[49] Cf. Hughes, *A History of the Church,* II, 131-138, 241.

[50] Council of Bourges (1031), c. 24—Mansi, XIX, 506; Council of Rheims (1049), c. 8—Mansi, XIX, 741; Council of Tours (1060), c. 10—Mansi, XIX, 98; Council of Toulouse (1119), c. 10—Mansi, XXXI, 227; Council of Naples (1110), c. 21—Mansi, XXI, 265; Council of Winchester (c. 1076), c. 12—Mansi, XX, 460; Council of London (1102), c. 11—Mansi, XX, 1151; Council of London (1138), c. 14—Mansi, XXI, 513.

[51] Hyland, *Excommunication,* pp. 35, 37.

[52] Council of Tours (1060), c. 10—Mansi, XIX, 928.

[53] Council of Bourges (1031), c. 24—Mansi, XIX, 506.

[54] *Ep. ad clerum et plebem Florentinum*—c. 11, C. XVI, q. 1; J L, n. 4552.

Gratian" and the general and particular councils held up to that time.

Article II. The Monastic Rules

The monastic founders in Spain also required the monks to remain in their monasteries.[55] St. Isidore of Seville (+636) in his "Rule for Monks" said that the enclosure of the monastery should be guarded, and that the gardens should be within the monastery lest the monks be given occasion to wander.[56] He enumerated among the crimes to be punished with more than three days "excommunication" from the community, the leaving of one's monastery without permission for a half day or more.[57]

St. Fructuosus, Archbishop of Braga (d. 665), in his *Regula Communis,* said that a monk who had left his monastery should not, even in charity, be received in another, but should, with hands bound behind his back, be led back to his own monastery. If he had returned to the world, he and all those who received him were excommunicated, and none of the faithful were allowed to associate with him or with his co-operators. On his return to the monastery he was to take the last place.[58]

Benedictine monasticism was spread in Gaul through the efforts of St. Boniface (c. 675-754). In the latter part of the tenth and in the eleventh century the center of Benedictine monasticism was Cluny. This same period also saw the founding of the Camaldolese (c. 1012), the Carthusian (1084) and the Cistercian (c. 1113) Orders, all of them following in varied forms the Benedictine rule.

These new orders observed the general legislation of the Benedictine rule that monks who had left the monastery had to be received back at least three times. Their statutes also indicated the penances to be imposed by the abbots and the chapters and the varied ceremonies for the readmission of such monks; and, finally, they determined the place the returned monk was to occupy in the order, according to the amount of time that he had been out of the

[55] *Regula S. Leandri, Ep. Hispalensis,* c. 16—*MPL,* LXXII, 889.
[56] C. 1—*MPL,* LXXXIII, 869.
[57] C. 17—*MPL,* LXXXIII, 885.
[58] C. 20—*MPL,* LXXXVII, 1127.

monastery.[59] One divergence, however, is found among the Carthusians. The superior and his council were to consider if the number of the monks, the utility of the house, or the salvation of the monk demanded that they receive him back; otherwise he was to be given permission to go to another religious house in which he could save his soul.[60]

[59] *S. P. Benedicti Regula cum Commentariis,* c. 29—*MPL,* LXVI, 523-534; *Statuta Ordinis Carthusiensis,* c. LXXVII — Holstensius, *Codex Regularum Monasticarum et Canonicarum collectus olim a S. Benedicto Arianensi* (ed. M. Brockie, 6 tomes in 3 vols., Augustae Vindelicorum, 1759), Tom. II, 331; *Constitutiones Congregationis Camaldulensis,* c. XXXIX—*Holstensius, op. cit.,* II, 238, 239.

[60] *Statuta Ordinis Carthusiensis,* c. LXXVII—*Holstensius, op. cit.,* II, 331; *Consuetudines Guigonis I,* c. LXXVII—*MPL,* CLIII, 749.

CHAPTER IV

GRATIAN TO THE COUNCIL OF TRENT (1140-1545)

THE period between the "Decree of Gratian" (1140) and the "Decretals of Gregory IX" (1234) is short, but it contains numerous enactments in regard to apostates and fugitives. This period saw the founding of the military and mendicant orders and the renaissance of the Canons Regular. The "Decree of Gratian" was a private collection and all laws found in it retained the particular or general binding force of their original promulgation. The papal laws of this period were general or particular, the latter being considered as normative for similar cases, all however obtaining the force of universal law by promulgation in the "Decretals of Gregory IX."[1]

In a response to the Bishop of Beauvais, Alexander III (1159-1181) said that, if the monk in the case had been offered in the monastery by his parents, or had ratified his profession after he was fourteen years of age, he was to be compelled to return to the same monastery or to go to another religious institute.[2] Writing to the Bishop of Huesca and the Prior of St. Mary of Saragossa, the same Pope stated that, if the nun in the case had not entered the monastery through fear of death, or if she had later ratified her profession, she was to be compelled by censure to reassume the habit.[3]

Addressing the archbishops and other prelates of France, Alexander III forbade them to receive Cistercians who wandered about without the permission of their abbots, and commanded the bishops, after having warned these fugitives to return to their monastery, to

[1] Van Hove, *Prolegomena*, n. 191-207.

[2] C. 11, X, *de regularibus et transeuntibus ad religionem*, III, 31; J L, n. 10604.

[3] C. 1, X, *de his quae vi metusve causa fiunt*, I, 40; J L, n. 14041.

force them to do so by ecclesiastical censures which admitted of no appeal.[4]

Innocent III (1198-1216) in his responses to various bishops stated that religious were to be forced to observe the profession they had made. Writing to the Bishop and Chapter of Traú, suffragan see of Spalato in the Kingdom of Hungary, he said that if one had made his profession while he was out of his mind but later ratified it he was to be forced to stay in the monastery.[5]

In an instruction to the Bishop of Aachen he said that a cleric who took the habit of a canon on his deathbed was to be forced to observe the canonical life if he recovered.[6] To the Abbot of Afligeim and Master R., Pastor of Tenis and Gilbert, Canon of Utrecht, he said that one could leave during the time of probation before profession, without being considered an apostate. But if one had taken the habit of a novice with the intention of changing his whole life, at least he had to go to a less severe order and not return to the world.[7] Lastly, writing to the Archbishop of Auch, he lamented the fact that monks, canons and other regulars of this ecclesiastical province were living outside of their monasteries, engaging in prohibited work and collecting money for themselves. He directed the Archbishop to warn these monks to return to their monasteries and to give the collected money to their prelates for the use of the house. If the religious prelates neglected to demand this, after a warning from the archbishop, they were to be compelled to do so by suspension from office and benefice, without appeal.[8]

Honorius III (1216-1227), wrote two instructions on this matter. In the first he answered the question of the Archbishop of Tours as to what was to be done with apostates who, while they were in custody, could not be induced by threats or by kindness to reassume the monastic habit. The pope said they were to be put in prison

[4] *Appendix, Conc. Lat. III,* pars XXVII, *Ne clericus vel monachus,* cap. 6—c. 7, X, *de regularibus et transeuntibus ad religionem,* III, 31; Mansi, XXII, 374.

[5] C. 15, X, *de regularibus et transeuntibus ad religionem,* III, 31.

[6] C. 17, X, *de regularibus et transeuntibus ad religionem,* III, 31.

[7] C. 20, X, *de regularibus et transeuntibus ad religionem,* III, 31.

[8] C. 7, X, *de officio iudicis ordinarii,* I, 31.

under severe custody, so that they would have nothing but a miserable life, until they repented of their wickedness.[9] In the second instruction, to the Archbishop of Lyons, the pope said that if an apostate had received any orders while he was an apostate from the religious life he could not, without a dispensation from the Roman Pontiff, exercise the orders thus received, even after he had come back and done penance.[10]

Thus stood the law when Gregory IX (1227-1241) ascended the throne of Peter. The "Decretals of Gregory IX" contain one other reference to apostates. It is a decree of Gregory IX himself concerning the superiors of apostates. He required that abbots and priors *every year* seek after those who had illicitly left and also those who had been dismissed. If these religious could, according to the rule, be taken back, the superiors were to be compelled after a warning to receive them back, without prejudice to the discipline of the order. But if the order did not permit this, the pope directed that they be taken care of in a fitting place or in another monastery of the same order, where they could do penance. But if these apostate and dismissed religious remained obstinate they were to be excommunicated, and the excommunication was to be published by the prelates of the churches until the religious returned to their monasteries.[11]

In the synodal statutes of Odo, Bishop of Toul (1193), one reads in canon 6 that apostates were to be excommunicated each Sunday in all the parish churches, and if the apostates had taken wives, the wives and families were also to be excommunicated, as also were all who in any way associated with them.[12] The Council of Paris (1212) stated that if it came to the knowledge of the prelates that apostate monks were living as lay people, the latter wherever they were found, were to be excommunicated by the priests of the place and shunned by all.[13]

[9] C. 5, X, *de apostatis et reiterantibus baptisma,* V, 9.

[10] C. 6, X, *de apostatis et reiterantibus baptisma,* V, 9.

[11] C. 24, X, *de regularibus et transeuntibus ad religionem,* III, 31.

[12] Mansi, XXII, 649.

[13] Pars II, cap. 14—Mansi, XXII, 829; cf. also Council of Rouen (1214), pars II, cap. 14—Mansi, XXII.

With the promulgation of the "Decretals of Gregory IX" in 1234 there came into existence an authentic collection of universal laws that in the main remained in force up until the present Code of 1918. The laws affecting apostates and fugitives may thus be summarized. If anyone who had freely entered upon the monastic life, or who had been tacitly professed,[14] or who had been put in a monastery by his parents, or who, though he had entered under duress, later ratified his profession, gave up his profession, he was to be compelled to return to his monastery, and hand over all his acquired possessions to the superior for the use of the house. If he remained obstinate he was to be excommunicated by condemnatory sentence, shunned by all, and even put into prison, until he came to his senses. Superiors were obliged to seek out the fugitive or apostate religious annually, and in all charity had to receive him back when he returned repentant, if the discipline of the institute permitted it; otherwise superiors had to provide for him elsewhere. If the apostate had received orders during his apostasy from the religious life, the orders could not be exercised until a dispensation had been obtained from the pope.

Since there existed a universal law in the "Decretals of Gregory IX" very little legislation emanated from the Holy See during the subsequent period prior to the Council of Trent, though some of the papal constitutions dealt with matters pertaining to the individual religious institutes.

Martin IV (1281-1285) stated that if a mendicant, on pretext of permission to transfer to a non-mendicant order, began to wander about, he was to be warned, and even if he had permission to transfer he was to return within fifteen days to the order to which he belonged. If he neglected to do so within the specified period of fifteen days, he was to be considered a notorious excommunicated apostate from the religious life and was to be laid hold of by anyone even by invoking the secular arm if necessary.[15]

[14] Tacit profession by remaining in the monastery for one year was admitted by popes and councils.—Frey, *The Act of Religious Profession*, pp. 27, 28.

[15] C. 1, *de regularibus et transeuntibus ad religionem*, III, 8, in Extravag. com.

To put a check on the possibility for religious to wander about Boniface VIII (1294-1303), under penalty of excommunication to be incurred *ipso facto,* forbade all monks to put off the habit.[16] This *latae sententiae* excommunication remained in force down to 1918, so that an apostate regular who put off his habit incurred this excommunication *ipso facto,* even when a *ferendae sententiae* excommunication for obstinacy in his apostate status was not inflicted in the case.

Clement V (1305-1313) in the Ecumenical Council of Vienne (1311-1312) met another situation. Certain monks who had tired of regular observance had left their monasteries and were wandering about the courts of princes. Unless their superiors gave them the money they demanded, they conspired against them, betrayed them, caused them to be put into prison and the monasteries to be burned, even helping the princes to seize the goods of the monastery. Against these monks the pope inflicted a *latae sententiae* excommunication, and urged superiors to compel them to remain away from the courts of princes.[17]

Certain monks had gone abroad to places where there were relatively few Catholics. Due to their ignorance and inexperience they preached error. John XXII (1316-1334) directed superiors not to appoint such men for these missions, and stated that no monks should go to these places without letters from their superiors; the pope furthermore directed the prelates of those places to treat them as apostates from the religious life and to put them in prison if they did not present such letters.[18]

In the "Constitutions" of Benedict XII (1334-1342), one finds

[16] C. 2, *ne clerici vel monachi saecularibus negotiis se immisceant,* III, 24, in VI°.

[17] C. 12, n. 5—c. 1, § 5, *de statu monachorum,* III, 10, in Clem; Schroeder, *Disciplinary Decrees of the General Councils,* p. 426. "Though [this decree aiming at Benedictine reform] does not contain the formula of conciliar approval, there can be no doubt that its main provisions are based on conciliar material."—Schroeder, *op. cit.,* p. 428; cf. also Müller, *Das Konzil v. Vienne* (Münster, 1934), pp. 569-573.

[18] C. 2, *de regularibus et transeuntibus ad religionem,* III, 8, in Extravag. com.; *Bull. Rom. Taur.,* IV, 310.

a repetition of the obligation of superiors to seek their apostate and fugitive subjects annually, and to receive them back if it can be done without prejudice to the discipline of the order. If they were incorrigible, then these apostates and fugitives were to be separated from the rest of the community and nobody was to speak to them without the permission of the superior.[19]

This is the last universal legislation on the subject of unlawful departure from a religious institute that emanated from the Holy See until the time of the Council of Trent.

The particular councils within the period between "The Decretals of Gregory IX" and the Council of Trent repeated the prohibition against regulars leaving their monasteries without permission, even for the purpose of study.[20] These councils stressed two points. First, superiors were bound to seek their apostate subjects, to receive them back and to refrain from excessive penalties,[21] the Council of Salzburg (1281) enacting the suspension from the administration of temporalities for non-compliance after a warning.[22] Secondly, benefices, dignities and offices with or without the care of souls were not to be conferred on apostates or fugitives from religious institutes [23] the appointment being invalid,[24] and the one making the appoint-

[19] Const. 38—Mansi, XXV, 1031.

[20] Council of Buda (1279), cc. 64, 66—Mansi, XIV, 203; Council of Florence (1346), *De statu monachorum*—Mansi, XXVI, 50; Venetian Synodicon of St. Lawrence Justinian (c. 1450), cc. 29, 38—Mansi, XXXIa, 346, 361; Council of Cologne (1536), pars X, c. 11—Mansi, XXXII, 1282.

[21] Council of Mainz (1259), *De statu monachorum*—Mansi, XXIII, 999; Council of Cologne (1260), cc. 11, 18—Mansi, XXIII, 1026, 1027; Council of Salzburg (1274), c. 2—Mansi, XXIV, 137; Council of Prague (1346), *De statu monachorum*—Mansi, XXVI, 88.

[22] C. 6—Mansi, XXIV, 399.

[23] Council of Lambeth (1281), c. 19—Mansi, XXIV, 416; Council of Bergamo (1311), rub. 31—Mansi, XXV, 509; Council of Ravenna (1311), rub. 22—Mansi, XXV, 461; Council of Tarragona (1329), c. 4—Mansi, XXV, 839; Council of Albi (1368), c. 72—Mansi, XXVI, 517; Venetian Synodicon (c. 1450), c. 38—Mansi, XXXIa, 361; Council of Cologne (1538), pars X, cap. 15—Mansi, XXXII, 1244.

[24] Provincial Constitutions of Aquileia (1339), *De Apostatis non recipiendis*—Mansi, XXV, 1123.

ment *ipso facto* incurring excommunication[25] or suspension from office.[26]

In England excommunicated apostates from the religious life had at times succeeded in becoming officials of the archdeacons and in celebrating the divine services in parish churches. A Synod of London (1399) asked the king that each diocesan be given power in his diocese to take hold of and put such apostates into prison if they refused to return to their monasteries.[27] Some of the superiors in England had given their subjects permission to live alone at churches. The "Constitutions of the Province of York," revised (c. 1518) and promulgated by Thomas Cardinal Wolsey, Archbishop of York, ordained that they be given a companion or be recalled. Superiors who in the future gave this permission were to be fined 40 shillings sterling and the religious thus wandering about were to be considered as apostates from the religious life.[28]

Among the constitutions of one of the first reform popes, Julius II (1503-1513), is found one which contains ordinances for the good government of the Benedictine Congregation of monks, of St. Mary of Mount Olivet. This constitution directed the superiors of this congregation to seize all such monks who had apostatized or were wandering about and to put them into prison, compelling them by censures and other remedies to return to regular observance, and by calling in the help of the secular arm if that proved necessary. All who took in an apostate were bound, within three days after they found out that the monk was an apostate, to return him to his monastery, otherwise they were under an excommunication reserved to the Holy See.[29]

Thus at the time of the Council of Trent the universal law regarding apostates and fugitives from the religious life consisted of the law as found in the "Decretals of Gregory IX" with the addition of the *latae sententiae* excommunication for doffing the religious habit, as enacted by Pope Boniface VIII.

[25] Council of Bergamo (1311), rub. 13—Mansi, XXV, 509.

[26] Council of Ravenna (1311), rub. 22—Mansi, XXV, 461.

[27] C. 22—Mansi, XXVI, 926.

[28] Lib. III, c. 10—Mansi, XXXVa, 197.

[29] Julius II, const. *Etsi ad universos*, 4 iun. 1507, §§ 21, 22—*Bull. Rom. Taur.*, V, 444-455.

CHAPTER V

THE COUNCIL OF TRENT
(1545-1563)

In the period between the Decretals and the Council of Trent the Church suffered by the residence of her supreme head at Avignon, and by the division of her members by the Great Schism of the West. Abuses crept in, especially nepotism and the appointment of unworthy laymen to the bishoprics, with the consequent lowering of the moral level of the clergy. The closing decades of this period saw the beginnings of the so-called Reformation, started, be it noted, by an apostate friar, Martin Luther, who attempted marriage with an apostate nun.

Nearly thirty years after Luther's break with the Church the counter-reformation was launched by Pope Paul III (1534-1549) in the opening of the Council of Trent in 1545. In a reform decree of the sixth session of the Council it was stated that if a regular living outside his monastery committed a crime he could be punished and corrected by the local ordinary, who in such a case acted as a delegate of the Holy See.[1] The Council did not consider the question of regulars *ex professo* until its twenty-fifth and last session, held on December 3 and 4, 1563.

In 1549 the Council of Trent was forced to prorogue its sessions due to the opposition of the emperor. Meanwhile provincial and local councils enacted laws with regard to the unlawful departure of religious from their institutes. A diocesan synod held at Trier (1548) stated that apostates of both sexes were to be returned to their own monasteries. Furthermore subjects of this diocese, of whatsoever rank or dignity, were not permitted to receive, favor or protect apostates, or give them the care of souls or any office in the Church; they were obliged to admonish the apostates to return to their profession.[2]

[1] Conc. Trident., sess. VI, *de ref.*, c. 3.

[2] Edicta 7, 8—Mansi, XXXII, 1350.

In the next year, 1549, three provincial councils were held, at Trier, at Cologne and at Mainz. The Council of Trier extended to the whole province the edicts of the diocesan synod of the previous year.[3] The Council of Cologne likewise forbade the receiving or favoring of apostates of both sexes under penalty of *ipso facto* incurred excommunication,[4] and under the same penalty forbade anyone to permit them to administer the sacraments or to exercise any power in the Church.[5] The apostates were commanded to leave their false spouses and their concubines, if they had any, and to give up their unlawful occupations and return to their monasteries to do penance [6] and to seek absolution from their excommunication through the Apostolic See, or through those who were delegated to grant it.[7] Some apostates claimed to have dispensations, others had deceitfully obtained them. The bishops of the province were ordered to examine the rescripts after consulting the superiors of such religious. But if the religious had already put off the habit, they had to reassume it and stay in their monasteries until the bulls were examined, otherwise they were to be considered as notorious apostates, to be shunned by all, to be taken into custody by the civil magistrate and handed over to their superiors with all their goods.[8]

The Council of Mainz admonished superiors to seek after and bring back those who had left their monasteries. All ecclesiastical persons were to warn such religious in their district to return to their monastery within one month, or within that time to present the bulls of their dispensation for examination. If the religious refused to obey, the ecclesiastics were to denounce them to the bishops who would compel them by censure to return to regular observance. Moreover, superiors were not to keep such religious from returning by imposing on them more severe penalties than those which were enacted in the canons. Violation of this duty on the part of supe-

[3] Decr. 12—Mansi, XXXII, 1451.

[4] C. 1—Mansi, XXXII, 1383.

[5] C. 4—Mansi, XXXII, 1384.

[6] C. 6—Mansi, XXXII, 1385.

[7] C. 7—Mansi, XXXII, 1385.

[8] C. 11—Mansi, XXXII, 1388.

riors entailed for them the penalty of suspension both *a divinis* and also from the administration of spiritual and temporal goods.[9]

A council of the clergy of Scotland, which intended to correct abuses and check the inroads of Presbyterianism in that country, was held at Edinburgh in 1549. In this Council it was commanded that superiors use all diligence to seek and reclaim their apostates and fugitives. For this purpose they were to call on the help of the ordinaries of the places where the religious were, and if this was not enough the ordinaries were to ask the help of the secular power.[10]

During the reign of Mary (1553-1558) as Queen of England, Pope Julius III (1550-1555) sent Reginald Cardinal Pole to England as Papal Legate and as Archbishop of Canterbury. At a council of the Province of Canterbury held under his presidency in 1557 it was ordained that superiors were bound to receive back in all charity, the religious who had left their monasteries, except those who in the judgment of the bishop had conspired or whom it was foreseen would conspire in the death of their superiors or confrères. A religious could be judged to have the proper spirit in returning to his monastery if he humbly accepted whatever place or rank was assigned to him, or if he could prove by the testimony of witnesses that for one year prior to his return he had lived respectably and had nurtured the intention of returning. If a religious left his monastery a second time, then superiors were in no way bound to take him back.[11]

Pope Julius III reconvened the Council of Trent in May 1551, but due to the presence of the Protestant troops near Trent the Council was again prorogued in April of the following year. In the reform decrees of the fourteenth session of the Council it was stated that, in order to avoid any occasion of apostasy or of wandering about when permission to transfer to another order was given, it was understood that the regular was to remain in the Order to which he had transferred and perpetually in the cloister under obedience to his superior.[12]

[9] C. 78—Mansi, XXXII, 1428.
[10] Act. 10—Mansi, XXXVa, 436.
[11] *De recipiendis apostatis*—Mansi, XXXVa, 501.
[12] Conc. Trident., sess. XIV, *de ref.*, c. 11.

In 1555 Paul IV (1555-1559) ascended the papal throne. He was a reformer but wanted reform without a Council and apart from the interference of secular princes. On July 20, 1558, he published the constitution *Postquam,* which was directed against only apostate religious.[13] This constitution was quite sweeping in its enactments. The pope stated that all those who had made profession in any order and were living outside their cloisters on any pretext, and had not fulfilled the requirements of law, were deprived of any benefice and the revenues therefrom and of all academic degrees whether civil or ecclesiastical. They were moreover rendered perpetually incapable of receiving the same and were suspended from the exercise of all orders. The benefices which had thereby become vacant were to be filled according to law. Any appointment of an apostate or of a fugitive to a benefice in the future was invalid; and if a patron presented an apostate for a benefice the presentation was invalid and the patron lost his right of presentation for that time. All persons of whatever rank or dignity in the Church or State who received or helped apostates were to be excommunicated after a warning. Superiors and local ordinaries were to compel the apostates to return even by using corporal penances and, if it proved necessary, by calling in the help of the civil power; they also were to publish the excommunication of those who did not return. Apostates who refused to return to their monasteries were to wear a black biretta with two white stripes around its circumference. If they were found without it they could be forced under penalties to wear it by ecclesiastical and civil magistrates and judges.[14]

Two years later Pius IV (1559-1566) revoked the constitution of Paul IV because of the confusion and harm to souls that it was causing. He absolved the religious from the penalties they had incurred, and dispensed them from any irregularities. All cases were

[13] Schmalzgrueber, *Ius Canonicum Universum* (5 tomes in 12 vols., Romae, 1843-1845), Lib. III, tit. XXXI, n. 270.

[14] Paul IV, const. *Postquam,* 20 iul. 1558—*Codex Iuris Canonici Fontes cura Emi Petri Card. Gasparri editi* (9 vols., Vols. VII, VIII, IX ed. *cura et studio Emi Justiniani Card. Serédi,* Romae [postea Civitate Vaticana]: Typis Polyglottis Vaticanis, 1923-1939), n. 93 (hereafter to be cited as *Fontes*); cf. also *Bull. Rom. Taur.,* VI, 538-543.

reserved to the Holy See. The apostates were obliged to present their permissions and dispensations, within six months from the date of the publication of this constitution, to the appointed judges under penalty of *ipso facto* falling back into the penalties.[15]

In November of the same year Pius IV issued another constitution which ordained that all the property and goods that regulars had acquired either by illicit occupations or in any way contrary to the sacred canons, in a word all the property unlawfully acquired by apostate religious, belonged to the Apostolic Camera, and this property could and had to be collected and appropriated as perpetually belonging to the Camera, no matter where the apostate had died or to whom the property had been willed.[16]

In his constitution on the reform of the Sacred Penitentiary, Pius IV stated that in the permission to transfer to another Order the clause that the religious was bound to remain in the monastery of the new obedience was always to be appended. Moreover the Major Penitentiary was not to grant absolution to apostates except on the condition that they immediately returned to their own monastery or entered another of equal or of stricter observance and remain there perpetually.[17]

Pius IV reconvened the twice prorogued Council of Trent in 1562. It took up the question of regulars in its last session held on December 3-4, 1563. The Council ordained that no regular could without the permission of his superior subject himself to any prelate, prince or university or any other person or place. Regulars were not to be allowed to leave their convents on the pretext[18] of going to their

[15] Const. *Sedis Apostolicae,* 3 apr. 1560—*Fontes,* n. 96; *Bull. Rom. Taur.,* VII, 15-18.

[16] Const. *Decens esse,* 5 nov. 1560, § 2—*Bull. Rom. Taur.,* VII, 78, 79.

[17] Const. *In sublime,* 4 maii 1562, §§ 8, 9—*Bull. Rom. Taur.* VIII, 193-197.

[18] Pretext here meant either a light cause or no cause at all, but did not include the case wherein the religious had a grave cause for leaving his monastery and for going to his superior.—Benedictus XIV, *De Synodo Dioecesana,* Lib. XIII, c. XI, n. 14; Ferraris, *Prompta Bibliotheca,* s. v. "Apostasia," n. 32; Matthaeucci, *Officialis curiae regularis ad optime defendenda suae religionis iura in curia ventilanda satis instructus* (2 tomes in 1 vol., Romae, Venetiis, 1702-1703), I, p. 63, n. 17, hereafter to be cited as *Officialis Curiae Regularis.*

superiors unless they had actually sent for them. Whoever was found without this permission in writing was to be punished by the local ordinary as a deserter of his institute. Those who went to the universities for studies were to live in convents, otherwise the ordinary could proceed against them.[19] Nuns were forbidden to leave their monastery even for a short time under any pretext, except for a legitimate cause approved by the ordinary.[20]

Finally the Council declared that regulars who wanted to assert the nullity of their profession were to offer their claim only within the five years after profession. They were not to dare to put off the habit, or even with the habit to leave without the superior's permission. If they had already put off the habit they were not to be admitted to institute in any case, but were to be punished as apostates; meanwhile they did not enjoy the privileges of their institute.[21]

Thus it must be noted that the principal additions made by the Council of Trent to existing legislation on the unlawful departure of religious from their institutes were: A regular who committed a crime while he was outside of his monastery could be punished by the local ordinary; permission to transfer to another institute implied that the religious was to remain in the institute of his new obedience; a regular was not allowed to attend universities or to be subject to any prince or prelate without the permission of his superior; a regular was not to leave his monastery on the pretext of going to his superior; finally, those who wished to impugn their profession on the ground of nullity were to stay in the monastery, and the use of this option was granted only within the five years following the act of their profession.

[19] Conc. Trident., sess. XXV, *de regularibus,* c. 4.

[20] Conc. Trident., sess. XXV, *de regularibus,* c. 5.

[21] Conc. Trident., sess. XXV, *de regularibus,* c. 19.

CHAPTER VI

THE COUNCIL OF TRENT TO THE CODE (1563-1918)

The particular councils which were held within the century subsequent to the celebration of the Council of Trent restated in their statutes the previous legislation and especially that of the Council of Trent. They commanded monks and nuns not to leave their monasteries under any pretext, even of studies, otherwise they were to be punished by the local ordinary and sent back to their monasteries.[1] If they wished to impugn their profession on the ground of nullity they had to observe the law of the Council of Trent and could not leave the monastery before taking up the case.[2] They were not to be admitted to administer the sacraments, to perform sacred functions or to exercise the care of souls.[3] The Council of Salzburg (1569)

[1] Council of Salzburg (1569), const. XXX, c. 9—Mansi, XXXVIa, 228; Council of Besançon (1571), *Statuta religiosorum,* c. 2—Mansi, XXXVIb, 74; Council of Gnesen (1577), c. 20—Mansi, XXXVIb, 633; Council of Bordeaux (1583), c. 25—Mansi, XXXIVa, 788; Council of Rheims (1583), c. 19, nn. 11, 16—Mansi, XXXIVa, 703, 704; Council of Bourges (1584), tit. 37, cc. 9, 17—Mansi, XXXIVb, 920; Council of Aix (1585), *De Monasteriis* — Mansi, XXXVIb, 879; Council of Fermo (1590), c. 24, n. 1—Mansi, XXXVIb, 908; Council of Avignon (1594), tit. 53, 54—Mansi, XXXIVb, 1559-1562; Council of Amalfi (1597), *De Sanctimonialibus eorumque monasteriis,* c. 1—Mansi, XXXVb, 1150; Council of Narbonne (1609), c. 33—Mansi, XXXIVb, 1515; Council of Bordeaux (1624), cap. 17, c. 3—Mansi, XXXIVb, 1588.

[2] Council of Salzburg (1569), const. XXX, c. 6—Mansi, XXXVIa, 227; Council of Rouen (1581), *De Monasteriis,* n. 17—Mansi, XXXIVa, 656; Council of Tours (1583), c. 17—Mansi, XXXIVa, 846; Council of Aix (1583), *De Monasteriis*—Mansi, XXXIVb, 1004.

[3] Council of Salzburg (1569), const. XXX, c. 18—Mansi, XXXVIa, 233; Council of Gnesen (1577), lib. IV, *De Apostatis*—Mansi, XXXVIb, 763; Council of Cosenza (1579), sess. V, *De Apostatis*—Mansi, XXXVb, 959; Council of Aix (1585), *De Monasteriis*—Mansi XXXIVb, 1004; III Council of Mexico (1585), lib. III, tit. 13, § 20—Mansi, XXXIVb, 1123; Council of Benevento (1599), tit. 32, c. 1—Mansi, XXXVIb, 444.

alone made a departure from the previous legislation. It stated that superiors were not to be exacting and excessive in the application of penalties relative to those who returned within the two months prescribed by the council. If despite this the apostate was still fearful, he was to go to the local ordinary within the same two months and explain his case. But if he continued in his obstinacy he was to be excluded from the province, and each bishop was to notify the others of such apostates. Those who knowingly sheltered apostates for eight days after the two months which were given to them to return to their monasteries were excommunicated if they were ecclesiastics. If those who sheltered them were laymen they lost for the one instance the right of patronage and other ecclesiastical rights and were interdicted from entering a church for two months.[4]

From the sixteenth century the Church began to tolerate religious institutes the members of which took simple instead of solemn vows. The members of these institutes who unlawfully left with the intention of either perpetually or temporally deserting their institutes were not classed as apostates or fugitives, nor did they incur the penalties for unlawful departure from a religious institute, unless by special disposition of the Holy See such penalties were applied to them. The reason for this was the fact that prior to the Code those who took simple vows were not considered religious in the strict sense of regulars.[5] Moreover the penalties enacted for apostate and fugitive regulars were factors of an odious character in the law and hence did not apply to non-regulars in view of the general principle of law that odious things are to be restricted.[6] Therefore these penalties were not extended to those who were professed with only simple vows unless the Holy See expressly so provided to the contrary in some specific cases.

Pope Gregory XIII (1572-1585) in two constitutions directed to the Society of Jesus stated that, though the members took simple vows at their profession, those who apostatized were subject to ex-

[4] Const. XXX, cap. 21-24—Mansi, XXXVIa, 234-236.

[5] Vermeersch, *De Religiosis Institutis et Personis* (2. ed., 2 vols., Brugis: Beyaert, 1907), I, 64; Wernz, *Ius Decretalium*, Tom. III, pars II, n. 610; Molitor, *Religiosi Iuris Capita Selecta* (Ratisbonae: Pustet, 1909), pp. 173, 221.

[6] Reg. 15, R. J. in VI°.

communication and to the other penalties of apostates, and that only the Holy See and the superior general of the Society could grant absolution from these penalties. The superior general for a reasonable cause could dismiss them and dispense them from their vows, but an apostate could not contract a valid marriage before he had received this absolution and dismissal from the Society.[7]

Popes Gregory XIII [8] and Sixtus V (1585-1590) [9] restated the law of Pius IV [10] that the property which deceased apostates had unlawfully acquired belonged to the Apostolic Camera.

Pope Sixtus V, in an effort to put an end to monks' wandering about, published two constitutions on this subject.[11] In these constitutions he stated that religious who traveled in another province, or even in their own if they were not well known, were to present a written permission of their superiors, otherwise they could not be allowed to stay in a monastery. Even if they claimed they were going to the Holy See to seek redress for injuries inflicted by their superior, and hence could not get the letter, they were not to be received unless they showed a testimonial that they had asked for permission and that it had been denied. Superiors who received such monks without the necessary letters incurred the privation of electoral rights, of offices, of dignities and of honors and were perpetually rendered incapacitated for them.

The Council of Trent had forbidden religious under any pretext to leave their monastery to go to superiors unless they had sent for them.[12] Among these superiors there was also included the Holy See. A decree of the newly constituted *Sacra Congregatio super consultationibus regularium* stated that if a religious for a light or rash cause

[7] Const. *Quanto fructuosius,* 1 febr. 1583, §§ 2, 3—*Bull. Rom. Taur.,* VIII, 406-409; *Fontes,* n. 150; const. *Ascendente Domino,* 25 maii 1584, §§ 17, 22—*Bull. Rom. Taur.,* VIII, 457-465; *Fontes,* n. 153.

[8] Const. *Officii nostri,* 21 ian. 1577, § 3—*Bull. Rom. Taur.,* VIII, 162-164.

[9] Const. *In conferendis,* 23 ian. 1590, § 17—*Bull. Rom. Taur.,* IX, 165-177.

[10] Const. *Decens esse,* 5 nov. 1560, § 2—*Bull. Rom. Taur.,* VII, 78, 79.

[11] Const. *Cum de omnibus,* 26 nov. 1587, § 7—*Bull. Rom. Taur.,* VIII, 951-955; *Fontes,* n. 163; const. *Ad Romanum spectat,* 21 oct. 1588, §§ 19, 20—*Bull. Rom. Taur.,* VIII, 455-460; *Fontes,* n. 164.

[12] Conc. Trident., sess. XXV, *de regularibus,* c. 4.

and without permission of his superior went to Rome for his case, he was to be sent back to be more severely punished by his superiors.[13] In a later case the Sacred Congregation of Bishops and Regulars upheld a religious who came directly to Rome with a companion, and annulled the sentence of apostasy passed on them by their superiors for leaving their monastery.[14]

Pope Clement VIII (1592-1605), in a decree on the reservation of faculties for the absolving of religious, enumerated among the offenses which the superior could reserve to himself apostasy from the religious institute when the religious left at night even without the intention of deserting. Superiors were to name confessors who could absolve from such a reservation when the confessor judged that he needed the faculty.[15]

To prevent monks from wandering about, Pope Clement revoked the grants of those who had received permission to live outside their monasteries, and ordered them to return to their monasteries. Those who went to Rome without the permission of the superior general or of the protector, as well as those who received them, were deprived of active and passive electoral rights for two years.[16] By the decree of March 20, 1601, it was permitted to go to Rome with the permission of the provincial, but all superiors were interdicted from mitigating or relaxing the above penalties.[17] The decree *Nullus omnino* and the decree of 1601 were repromulgated with some additions for the reform of the Servites. In this latter decree it was stated that a prior who unlawfully gave permission to a monk to stay outside of his

[13] S. C. Regularium, decr. *Quoniam nonnulli regularis vagandi studio,* 1587 —Matthaeucci, *Officialis Curiae Regularis,* Tom I, p. 66, n. 32.

[14] S. C. Ep. et Reg., *Ordinis Fratrum Discalceatorum S. Augustini Gravaminis,* 2 sept. 1672—Bizzarri, *Collectanea in usum Sacrae Congregationis Episcoporum et Regularium* (Romae, 1863), p. 300. Hereafter to be cited as Bizzarri, all references being to this edition.

[15] Decr. *Sanctissimus,* 26 maii 1593, § 1, n. 2, and § 3—*Fontes,* n. 177; Bizzarri, pp. 274, 275.

[16] Clement VIII, decr. *Nullus omnino,* 25 iul. 1599, §§ 13, 19—*Fontes,* n. 187; *Bull. Rom. Taur.,* X, 662-667. The active electoral right denotes the right to cast a ballot in an election; the passive electoral right signifies the right of receiving a vote in the capacity of an electoral candidate.

[17] *Bull. Rom. Taur.,* X, 667.

monastery *ipso facto* incurred suspension from office for six months. The prior could give his monks permission to go out only twice a week, but never on a feast day unless necessity urged it. A prior who received a monk from another monastery without asking to see and without reading his written permission incurred suspension from office for one month.[18]

In a response of the Sacred Congregation of Bishops and Regulars in a particular case it was stated that the Order of Our Lady of Mercy for the Redemption of Captives was bound, and was to be compelled, to take back an apostate who sought to return; but he was to be subject to the penalties of the sacred canons and their constitutions.[19] Similarly in the case of an apostate Capuchin, who was refused readmission because of a contagious disease (the rule of the order forbidding the readmission of apostates with a contagious disease), the Sacred Congregation of the Council decided that he must be taken back because his disease was not contagious as far as the community was concerned.[20]

In another decree published on the same day the Sacred Congregation declared that the time which an apostate spent outside the order was to be counted when determining his precedence in the order. This decision was reversed on May 2 of the same year.[21]

The mind of the Church after the Council of Trent on the question of apostates is summarized in a decree of the Sacred Congregation of the Council published at the command of Pope Urban VIII (1623-1644). This decree, in view of the danger of apostasy from religious institutes forbade superiors to grant permission to religious to transfer to a stricter institute unless they were sure that the second institute would receive them. The old legislation was restated, namely, that apostates and fugitives were to be compelled by the

[18] Clement VIII, decr. *Nullus omnino,* 22 aug. 1604, §§ 35, 60, 63—*Bull. Rom. Taur.,* X, 662-673.

[19] S. C. Ep. et Reg., *Ordinis B. M. V. de Mercede,* 10 febr. 1604—*Fontes,* n. 1630.

[20] S. C. C., *Capuccinorum,* 31 ian. 1682—*Analecta Juris Pontificii,* XXVI (1886), 708 (hereafter to be cited as *AJP*).

[21] S. C. C., *Praeeminentiae,* 31 ian., 2 maii 1682—*AJP,* XXVI (1886), 705, 706.

local ordinaries to return to the monastery and were to be sought after and received by their superiors. The penalties inflicted or to be inflicted were to be remitted if apostates in cisalpine territory returned to their monasteries within four months and if apostates in transalpine territory did so within eight months from the publication of this decree. If anyone did anything contrary to the prescripts of this decree, or altered them in any way, or undermined them, he *ipso facto* incurred the privation of all offices, of both active and passive electoral rights, and the perpetual incapacity for these in the future. These penalties were reserved to the Holy See and the use of any and all power on the part of major superiors with regard to these penalties was interdicted.[22] This decree was referred to in three later decrees of the same Congregation.[23] In the last of these decrees, which was published at the command of Pope Innocent XII (1691-1700), the Pope confirmed the decree of September 21, 1624, and also the decree of Gregory IX, to the effect that superiors were bound to seek their apostate subjects *annually*.[24]

Because of the danger of religious' wandering about Innocent X (1644-1655),[25] Benedict XIII (1724-1730)[26] and Clement XII (1730-1740)[27] published constitutions forbidding the transfer of regulars to another order, at least when it was done without permission.

The decree of Urban VIII had remitted the penalties of apostates in cisalpine territory if they returned within four months and of apostates in transalpine territory if they returned within eight months. This practice was followed by the Popes on the occasion of the jubilee years, as is clear from the constitution of Pope Benedict XIV (1740-1758), the greatest of canonist popes, who declared that he

[22] S. C. C., decr. 21 sept. 1624, §§ 3, 4, 5, 13—*Bull. Rom. Taur.*, XIII, 202-205; *Fontes*, n. 2454.

[23] S. C. C., *Limana*, 10 mart. 1629—*Fontes*, n. 2505; *Minimorum*, 15 mart. 1636—*Fontes*, n. 2579; *Instantibus*, 24 iul. 1694—*Fontes*, n. 2942.

[24] C. 24, X, *de regularibus et transeuntibus ad religionem*, III, 31.

[25] Const. *Iniuncti nobis*, 25 sept. 1646—*Bull. Rom. Taur.*, XV, 483-485.

[26] Const. *Licet Sacra*, 13 febr. 1726—*Bull. Rom. Taur.*, XVII, 320-322.

[27] Const. *Emanarunt*, 27 mart, 1738—*Bull. Rom. Taur.*, XXIV, 356-358.

was following the practice of his predecessors Urban VIII, Clement X, Innocent XII and Benedict XIII. In the year of jubilee the faculty of absolving from the penalties for apostatsy was given to the superiors of those apostates who returned to their monasteries within the time stated.[28]

In a constitution on the faculties of the Sacred Penitentiary, published by Benedict XIV, the Major Penitentiary was given the power to absolve apostates if he enjoined on them a fixed time to return to their monasteries under penalty of their reincidence into the penalty. He was also given power to condone, moderate or commute other penalties of either the common or the particular law incurred by apostates. If the case of an apostate was being discussed before the Apostolic Signatura, the Major Penitentiary could permit such a religious to transfer to another institute taking precautions against wandering, but he was never to allow such a religious to live perpetually in the world in secular dress.[29]

In a constitution referring to religious who impugned the validity of their profession or who sought the grant of a *restitutio in integrum*,[30] Benedict XIV restated the law of the Council of Trent,[31] namely, that their case was not to be taken up if they had left their monasteries. He added that they were not to leave their monasteries until they had obtained two comformable sentences of nullity relative to their profession, or a grant of *restitutio in integrum*, otherwise they incurred all the penalties of apostates.[32] In the nineteenth century

[28] Const. *Pastoris aeterni*, 12 ian. 1749—*Benedicti XIV Bullarium* (3 tomes bound in 4, Prati, 1845-1847), Tom. III, pars I, pp. 199, 200 (hereafter to be cited as *Bull. Ben.*).

[29] Const. *Pastor bonus*, 13 apr. 1744, § 33—*Bull. Ben.*, I, 354-363.

[30] *Restitutio in integrum* is an extraordinary remedy of the law by which a person who has been gravely damaged by a valid but rescissible act or transaction may, because of natural equity, be restored, through the ministry of a competent judge, to that status in which he was before he sustained damage. Cf. Feeney, *Restitutio in Integrum*, The Catholic University of America Canon Law Studies, n. 129 (Washington, D. C.: The Catholic University of America Press, 1941), p. 49.

[31] Conc. Trident., sess. XXV, *de regularibus*, c. 19.

[32] Const. *Si datam*, 4 mart. 1748, §§ 9, 13, 20—*Bull. Ben.*, II, 331-339, *Fontes*, n. 385.

this constitution was confirmed by Pope Pius IX (1846-1878), who determined the special process to be followed in such cases.[33]

A decree of the Sacred Congregation of Bishops and Regulars during the last year of the pontificate of Benedict XIV declared that a religious who had fled to another institute was to be sent back to his own superior unless he would be punished by him with such corporal punishments as perpetual imprisonment, death or the galleys, in which case he was to be allowed to stay in the monastery to which he had fled. If, however, on his return he would be punished only with ordinary penances, then he and the superior who did not send him back incurred the excommunication for apostates and the receivers of apostates, which excommunication was reserved to the Pope.[34]

The next legislation that must be considered is the Constitution *Apostolicae Sedis* of Pope Pius IX under date of October 12, 1869.[35] Since this constitution rearranged the law with regard to only the *latae sententiae* penalties of the common law, it did not affect the penalties for unlawful departure from a religious institute, because prior to the Code these were *ferendae sententiae* penalties. However, if the apostate had put off the habit, he incurred the *latae sententiae* excommunication enacted by Boniface VIII.[36] The constitution *Apostolicae Sedis* stated that penalties enacted for the internal government of religious institutes were not revoked by it. Hence Wernz,[37] Piatus Montensis[38] and the many authors cited by them claimed that this *latae sententiae* excommunication remained in force precisely because it referred to the internal government of religious institutes. On the other hand, Santi,[39] Avanzini,[40] Pennacchi[41] and

[33] Const. *Pecularibus,* 26 ian. 1856—Bizzarri, pp. 147-153.

[34] S. C. Ep. et Reg., *Ordinis S. Augustini,* 11 aug. 1758—Bizzarri, p. 365; *Fontes,* n. 1873.

[35] *Fontes,* n. 552.

[36] C. 2, *ne clerici vel monachi saecularibus negotiis se immisceant,* III, 24, in VI°.

[37] *Ius Decretalium,* III, n. 674.

[38] *Praelectiones Juris Regularis,* I, p. 209, q. 219, nota 6.

[39] *Praelectiones Juris Canonici* (4. ed., cura martini Leitner, 5 vols., Ratisbonae: Pustet, 1903-1905), Lib. III, tit. 31, n. 46.

[40] *De Constitutione Apostolicae Sedis* (Romae, 1874), n. 57.

[41] *Commentarium in Constitutione Apostolicae Sedis* (2 vols., Romae, 1885), II, p. 547.

others contended that the *latae sententiae* excommunication for putting off the religious habit was no longer in force by the common law, but was incurred only if it was found enacted in the constitutions of religious institutes.

The latest legislation before the time of the present Code with regard to apostasy from a religious institute was a decree of the Sacred Congregation of Religious on May 16, 1911. In this decree on the dismissal from religious orders and other religious institutes, apostasy from the order or institute as long as the religious had not returned to his monastery within three months after the day of his desertion was listed among the crimes punished with automatic dismissal. If a religious in sacred orders was dismissed he *ipso facto* incurred suspension; and superiors were obliged to notify the ordinary of the place of origin and the ordinary of the place where the dismissed religious in sacred orders was staying or intended to stay. Moreover, all dismissed religious could not be advanced to any orders, nor could they reenter the order or institute from which they had been dismissed, nor could they enter any other order or institute, without the permission of the Holy See.[42]

Two points are to be noted about this decree inasmuch as they constitute a departure from the previous legislation on apostasy from a religious institute. First, the decree included apostasy from a religious institute among the crimes punished with automatic dismissal. This decree was enacted during the period of the codification of the present law. In all the preparatory schemata of the Code apostasy even without another crime was punished with automatic dismissal. After the last schema this legal effect was suppressed.[43] In the present Code simple and unqualified apostasy from a religious institute is no longer listed as a crime which automatically effects the dismissal of the religious.[44] The second point to be noted in this decree is that dismissal was incurred not only by those who had

[42] S. C. de Rel., decr. *Quum singulae,* 16 maii 1918, nn. 18, b; 19; 20—*Acta Apostolicae Sedis,* III (1911), 235-238 (hereafter to be cited as *AAS*); *Fontes,* n. 4409.

[43] Larraona, "Quaestio Canonica,"—*CpR,* IV (1923), 174, nota 1.

[44] Canon 646, § 1.

apostatized from an order, but also by those who had deserted their religious institute even though they had been professed with simple vows. This was the first evidence of a general law to treat those with simple vows who unlawfully leave their religious institute in the same manner as apostate regulars.

The legislation of the decree *Quum singulae* was short-lived, for it was abolished by the law of the Code which came into effect on Pentecost Sunday, 1918. The Code for the first time certainly considered as religious in the strict sense even those who took only simple vows, and thus through a changed viewpoint applied to them the same legislation that it applied to regulars. It accepted the notions of apostates and fugitives as current in the previous legislation and applied them to all religious whether they took solemn or only simple vows. Apostasy, however, was made to apply only to those religious who are professed with perpetual vows.[45] On the other hand, the law of the Church on unlawful departure from religious institutes is now by the Code made to comprise also the members of societies whose members live in common without public religious vows. This law applies to them in their obligation to return to their society, in the obligations which rest upon them in view of their private vows, their promises, or their oath, in the obligations which they have by their constitutions, and in the obligations which their superiors have to seek them and receive them back. In less than a month after the Code became the law of the Church the Pontifical Commission for the Interpretation of the Canons of the Code, in answer to a doubt, declared that the penalties stated in canon 2386 for fugitive religious are incurred also by members of clerical societies whose members live in common without vows when they unlawfully desert their society though they have the intention of returning to it.[46]

Pius XI (1922-1939) on the occasion of the jubilee years of 1925, 1926, 1933 and 1934 gave faculties to penitentiaries and confessors for use in the internal forum to absolve from censures reserved

[45] Canon 644, § 1.

[46] P. C. I., 2-3 iun, 1918—*AAS,* X (1918), 347.

a iure to the ordinary.[47] Hence those apostates and fugitives (if the latter incurred excommunication according to their constitutions) whose excommunication was reserved to the ordinary, and not specifically to the major superior as major superior, could have been absolved in the internal forum, on the condition that the apostates within a fixed time, and the fugitives *quam primum,* returned to their institutes or societies, and this under penalty of incurring the same kind of censure from which they had been absolved.[48] On the occasion of the extraordinary jubilee of 1929 the Pope gave the faculty to absolve from all cases reserved by law with but two exceptions and did not make any mention of the person or authority to whom they were reserved.[49] Hence even those apostates and fugitives whose censure was reserved to their proper major superiors could have been absolved. The question of the use of the jubilee faculties will be treated later in connection with the explanation of the law on the remission of the penalties for apostasy and flight.

[47] Const. *Si umquam,* 15 iul. 1924, §§ VI, XVI, n. 1—*AAS,* XVI (1924), 309-316; const. *Servatoris Iesu Christi,* 25 dec. 1925, § 3—*AAS,* XVII (1925), 611-618; const. *Indicto a Nobis,* 31 ian. 1933—*AAS,* XXV (1933), 14-19; const. *Quod superiore,* 2 apr. 1934, § VIII, n. 3—*AAS,* XXVI (1934), 137-148.

[48] S. Poenit., 31 iul. 1924, § 9—*AAS,* XVI (1924), 339, 340; 28 febr. 1933, § 9—*AAS,* XXV (1933), 62.

[49] Pius XI, const. *Auspicantibus,* 6 ian. 1929—*AAS,* XXI (1929), 5-11.

PART II

CANONICAL COMMENTARY

CHAPTER VII

APOSTATES FROM RELIGIOUS INSTITUTES

Canon 644, § 1. Apostata a religione dicitur professus a votis perpetuis sive sollemnibus sive simplicibus qui e domo religiosa illegitime egreditur cum animo non redeundi, vel qui, etsi legitime egressus non redit eo animo ut religiosae obedientiae sese subtrahat.

§ 2. Malitiosus animus, de quo in § 1, iure praesumitur, si religiosus intra mensem nec reversus fuerit nec Superiori animum redeundi manifestaverit.[1]

APOSTASY from a religious institute is a crime in ecclesiastical law,[2] for it is an external violation of the ecclesiastical law which requires a religious to persevere in his religious institute unless he is lawfully dispensed,[3] and this violation is punished with ecclesiastical penalties.[4] The crime has two essential elements: The first consists in the *fact* that a religious who has made profession of perpetual

[1] Canon 644, § 1. An apostate from religion is one who, having made profession of perpetual vows, whether solemn or simple, unlawfully leaves the religious house with the intention of not returning, or who, with the intention of withdrawing himself from religious obedience, though he has lawfully left the house, does not return to it.

§ 2. The perverse intention, referred to in § 1, is legally presumed when the religious within a month has neither returned nor manifested to his superior his intention of returning. (Authorized English Translation.)

[2] Canon 2195, § 1.

[3] Canons 487; 488, n. 1; 594, § 1; 1311.

[4] Canon 2385.

vows, whether solemn or simple, deserts his religious institute; the second in the *intention* of not returning to the institute.[5]

A. The Fact: A Religious with Solemn or with Simple Perpetual Vows Deserts His Religious Institute

1. *Profession*

To be an apostate from a religious institute one must be a religious in the sense of canon 488, n. 7, *i. e.,* one who has vows in a religious institute approved as such by the Church. Approval by the Church, whether the approval be of pontifical or of diocesan character, is necessary to establish the religious institute as a moral person in the Church, and to confer on its members the rights and obligations of religious.[6] Therefore one is not an apostate from a religious institute if one deserts an organization [7] which has not been recognized by the Church as a religious institute, either through diocesan or pontifical approval.[8] Servants and others who are not members of the religious institute, but who live in the house of clerical religious and are subject to the superior,[9] do not become apostates from a religious institute by abandoning the house with the intention of not returning, for they are not members of the institute.

[5] Coronata, *Institutiones,* n. 642; Chelodi-Dalpiaz, *Ius Poenale et Ordo Procedendi in Iudiciis Criminalibus iuxta Codicem Iuris Canonici* (4. ed., Tridenti: Ardesi, 1935), n. 101 (hereafter to be cited as Chelodi-Dalpiaz, *Ius Poenale*); Cocchi, *Commentarium in Codicem Iuris Canonici* (5 vols. in 8, Vol. VIII [*De Delictis et Poenis*], 2 ed., Taurinorum Augustae: Marietti, 1928), VIII, n. 261 (hereafter to be cited as Cocchi, *De Delictis et Poenis*); Cappello, *Tractatus Canonico-Moralis De Censuris iuxta Codicem Iuris Canonici* (3. ed., Taurinorum Augustae: Marietti, 1933), n. 390 (hereafter to be cited as Cappello, *De Censuris*); Creusen-Garesché-Ellis, *Religious Men and Women in the Code* (3. English ed., Milwaukee: Bruce, 1940), n. 340.

[6] Orth, *The Approbation of Religious Institutes,* The Catholic University of America Canon Law Studies, n. 71 (Washington, D. C.: The Catholic University of America, 1931), pp. 76-78.

[7] *E. g.,* Tertiaries.

[8] Suarez, Tr. VIII, lib. III, c. II, n. 6; Reiffenstuel, *Jus Canonicum Universum* (5 tomes in 7, Parisiis, 1864-1870), Lib. V, tit. IX, n. 11; Schmalzgrueber, Lib. V, tit. IX. n. 12; Piatus Montensis, *Praelectiones Juris Regularis,* I, q. 216.

[9] Canon 514, § 1.

Women religious who desert their religious institute with the intention of not returning are apostates. This is the common opinion as expressed by the authors who explicitly include women,[10] and those who implicitly include them by making no distinction between men and women religious.[11] Canon 490 states that the dispositions concerning religious, even when expressed in the masculine gender, apply equally to women religious, except it appears otherwise from the context or from the nature of the case. To exclude women clearly violates the principle that "where the law does not distinguish, neither should we distinguish." Moreover, canon 645 imposes on the local ordinary and the regular superior the duty of seeing to the return of apostate and fugitive nuns *(moniales)*. The opinion of the few authors [12] who exclude women religious from subjection to the excommunication enacted in canon 2385 lacks extrinsic and intrinsic probability.[13]

[10] Ayrinhac-Lydon, *Penal Legislation in the New Code of Canon Law* (New York: Benziger Bros., 1936), n. 375; Chelodi-Dalpiaz, *Ius Poenale*, n. 101; Cocchi, *De Delictis et Poenis*, n. 261; Cappello, *De Censuris*, n. 389; Beste, *Introductio in Codicem* (Collegeville, Minn.: St. John's Abbey Press, 1938), p. 438; Coronata, *Institutiones*, n. 2189; Smith, *The Penal Law for Religious*, The Catholic University of America Canon Law Studies, n. 98 (Washington, D. C.: The Catholic University of America, 1935), pp. 95, 96.

[11] Blat, *Commentarium Textus Codicis Iuris Canonici*, Lib. II, Partes II et III, *Ius de Religiosis et Laicis Iuxta Codicis Ordinem* (3. ed., Romae: Apud Angelicum, 1938), nn. 646-655 (hereafter to be cited as *Ius de Religiosis*); Lib. V, *De Delictis et Poenis* (Romae: Collegio Angelico, 1924), n. 228 (hereafter to be cited as *De Delictis et Poenis*); Cocchi, *Commentarium*, Vol. IV, *De Religiosis et Laicis* (2. ed., Taurinorum Augustae, Marietti, 1926), nn. 140-143 (hereafter to be cited as *De Religiosis et Laicis*); Fanfani, *De Iure Religiosorum* (2. ed., Taurini, Romae: Marietti, 1925), nn. 491-494; Schaefer, *De Religiosis*, nn. 564-571; Vermeersch-Creusen, *Epitome Iuris Canonici* (3. ed., 3 vols., Mechliniae, Romae: Dessain, 1927-1928), I, nn. 746, 747; III, nn. 589, 590.

[12] Cerato, *Censurae Vigentes Ipso Facto a Codice Iuris Canonici Excerptae* (2. ed., Patavii: Typis Seminarii, 1922), pp. 102, 103; Cipollini, *De Censuris Latae Sententiae iuxta Codicem Iuris Canonici* (Taurini: Marietti, 1925), p. 179; Pistocchi, *I Canoni Penali del Codice Ecclesiastico Esposti e Commentati* (Torino, Roma: Marietti, 1925), pp. 309, 310. For a discussion of the opinion of Cerato and Cipollini cf. Smith, *The Penal Law for Religious*, pp. 95, 96.

[13] Smith, *The Penal Law for Religious*, p. 96.

To be an apostate from his religious institute the religious who deserts his religious institute must have made profession of the public perpetual vows, either solemn or simple, of obedience, chastity and poverty. The vows must be public, for public vows are required of the members of a religious institute.[14] They must be the three vows of obedience, chastity and poverty, for these are essential to the religious state.[15]

A question arises as to the status of those members of societies whose members live in common without vows who desert the society with the intention of not returning. Since canon 681 applies canon 645 *"congra congruis referendo"* to members of societies living in common without vows, and, since canon 645 expressly treats of apostates and fugitives, the notions of "apostate" and "fugitive" are applicable to members of those societies when they desert the society.[16] Since they do not make profession of the three public vows which are necessary to constitute them as religious they cannot be apostates in the strict sense, and therefore are not subject to the penalties of canon 2385.[17] They may be called apostates in the wide sense,[18] or *ad instar* apostates,[19] and are subject to any penalties which their constitutions may state.[20] But they may not be called

[14] Canon 488, n. 1.

[15] Canon 487; *supra*, p. 3.

[16] Blat, *Ius de Religiosis*, nn. 650, 654.

[17] Blat, *loc. cit.;* Schaefer, *De Religiosis*, n. 610; Vermeersch-Creusen, *Epitome*, I, n. 781; Biederlack-Führick, *De Religiosis* (Oeniponte: Rauch, 1919), n. 169; Goyeneche, *Iuris Canonici Summa Principia, De Religiosis* (Romae: Tip, Pol. "Cuore di Maria," 1938), n. 137; Toso, *Ad Codicem Juris Canonici Commentaria Minora* (5 vols., Romae: Jus Pontificium, 1920-1934), Lib. II, *De Personis*, pars I, tom. III, p. 240 (hereafter to be cited as Toso, *Commentaria Minora*); Voltas, "Consultationes,"—*CpR*, I (1920), 270-272; Maroto, "Annotationes,"—*CpR*, I (1920), 105, 106.

[18] Maroto, *loc. cit.*

[19] Schaefer, *De Religiosis*, n. 609.

[20] In the constitutions of the Pallottine Fathers suspension is automatically incurred, if the member is in sacred orders, which suspension is reserved to the immediate major superior.—*Constitutiones Piae Societatis Missionum* (Ratisbonae: Pustet [no date]), const. 205.

fugitives, because a fugitive leaves with the intention of returning,[21] and it is the intention which formally differentiates the apostate from the fugitive.[22] Coronata says that in societies whose members live in common without vows the crimes of apostasy and flight seem to coalesce and are prohibited under the same sanctions, *i. e.*, those which are invoked against fugitives. He says that it is absurd to punish one who leaves with the intention of returning and not punish one who leaves with the intention of not returning.[23] To avoid falling into this absurdity he includes under the term "fugitive" also those who, if they were true religious, would commit a crime specifically distinct from that of flight by leaving with the intention of not returning.

Since novices are without vows and therefore are not religious in the sense of canon 488, n. 7, and are juridically free to leave,[24] they cannot become apostates from a religious institute.[25] If a religious, in the case of his transfer to another religious institute, deserts the novitiate of the second institute in order to return to the institute in which he has taken vows,[26] he is not an apostate from his religious institute. If, however, he deserts the novitiate with the intention of not returning to his first institute, he is an apostate from his religious institute and becomes subject to the penalties. The superiors of his first institute are obliged to seek him and receive him back.[27]

Religious with temporary vows [28] who unlawfully desert the institute with the intention of not returning, are not apostates from a

21 Voltas, *loc. cit.*

22 *Infra,* pp. 62, 64, 73, 74.

23 *Institutiones,* n. 642.

24 Canon 571, § 1.

25 Schmalzgrueber, Lib. V, tit. IX, n. 13.

26 The vows remain during the novitiate in the second institute.—Canon 633, § 1.

27 *Infra,* p. 119.

28 It does not matter whether they are members of an institute in which only temporary vows or vows as long as the religious lives in the congregation are taken, or members of an institute in which temporary vows are taken for at least three years prior to perpetual profession.

religious institute.[29] The reason why the law does not include them seems to be the fact that, after the lapse of their vows they regain their juridical liberty.[30] Some authors say that they are compared to fugitives and are to be treated jurdically as fugitives.[31]

Goyeneche claims that the case is contained in the idea of a fugitive as a species is contained in its genus. He says that Santamaria concludes that such a religious does what the fugitive religious does, and even more, and also contends that the prohibition of applying penalties from one case to another [32] is not violated, since there is in this case a question of flight aggravated by another circumstance. This added circumstance is the intention of not returning.

But this seems to be a departure from the strict interpretation of the definition of a fugitive [33] which must be used in the application of penalties.[34] Moreover, it is the intention with which the religious leaves that specifically differentiates the crime of apostasy from that of flight.[35] The intention with which a fugitive leaves is

[29] Fanfani, *De Iure Religiosorum,* n. 491; Schaefer, *De Religiosis,* n. 566, Biederlack-Führich, *De Religiosis,* n. 169; Toso, *Commentaria Minora,* pars I, tom. III, p. 240; Coronata, *Institutiones,* n. 862; Vermeersch-Creusen, *Epitome,* I, n. 746; III, n. 589; Chelodi-Dalpiaz, *Ius Poenale,* n. 101; De Meester, *Juris Canonici et Juris Canonico-Civilis Compendium* (nova ed., 3 vols in 4, Brugis: Desclée, De Brouwer & Si, 1921-1928), n. 1054 (hereafter to be cited as De Meester, *Compendium*); Creusen-Garesché-Ellis, *Religious Men and Women in the Code,* n. 341; Pejska, *Ius Canonicum Religiosorum* (3. ed., Friburgi Brisgoviae: Herder, 1927), n. 20; Pruemmer, *Manuale Iuris Canonici,* q. 255; Woywod, *A Practical Commentary on the Code of Canon Law* (3. ed., 2 vols., New York: Wagner, 1929), I, n. 561; Berutti, *Institutiones Iuris Canonici* (Vols. I, III, VI, Taurini, Romae: Marietti, 1936-1938), III, *De Religiosis,* n. 156 (hereafter to be cited as Berutti, *De Religiosis*); Goyeneche, "Consultationes,"—*CpR,* XIV (1933), 257-259.

[30] Coronata, *loc. cit.;* Vermeersch-Creusen, *loc. cit.*

[31] Berutti, *loc. cit.;* Coronata, *loc. cit.;* Pejska, *loc. cit.;* Goyeneche, *loc. cit.*; Toso, *loc. cit.*; Vermeersch-Creusen, *loc. cit.* This is the opinion of Vermeersch and not of Creusen, the latter holding that they are not fugitives and citing the above opinion as that of Vermeersch.—Creusen-Garesché-Ellis, *Religious Men and Women in the Code,* n. 341.

[32] Canon 20.

[33] Canon 644, § 3.

[34] Canon 19.

[35] *Infra,* pp. 62, 73.

that of deserting the institute for a time only and of later returning to it.[36] Therefore it must be concluded that, since the religious with temporary vows who leaves with the intention of not returning has not the exact intention connoted by the concept of flight he is not a fugitive nor subject to the penalties enacted for fugitives.

2. The Egress

The Code distinguishes between those who unlawfully, *i. e.*, without permission, leave their religious house with the intention of not returning, and those who, though they have lawfully left the house, do not return to it and have the intention of not returning, but regards both as apostates. There is no real difference between them,[37] for when the religious who has lawfully left his religious house deserts the place assigned to him under obedience and forms the intention of not returning to this religious institute he is from that moment onward unlawfully outside his religious house with the intention of not returning to his religious institute.[38]

The Code speaks of the departure of the religious from the religious house. This is not to be taken strictly, since the authors agree that a religious who deserts his religious house or the place assigned to him under obedience in order to go to another house of his institute, or to the Holy See is not an apostate. Moreover, canon 645, § 1, in speaking of the obligation of apostates and fugitives to return does not say that they must return to the house which they left, but simply that they must return to their institute.

The crime of apostatsy is constituted by two elements: the fact of unlawful departure from the religious institute and the intention of not returning to it. Both elements are necessary. Therefore, if a religious has merely the intention of deserting his religious institute but in reality does not leave his religious house, he internally commits the sin of apostasy from his institute but he does not commit

[36] *Infra*, pp. 73-75.

[37] Beste, *Introductio in Codicem*, p. 437; Schaefer, *De Religiosis*, n. 565.

[38] When reference is made in this dissertation to unlawful departure from the religious house both cases will be included unless explicit indication is given to the contrary.

the external crime of apostasy from his institute. Likewise, if a religious is lawfully outside of his house, *i. e.*, in giving a mission, or in acting as a parochial vicar, or in supplying for a priest in a parish,[39] and decides to desert his religious institute, he does not become an apostate as long as he does not leave the place of his assignment.[40] It is only when he has been recalled to his religious house that his remaining outside of it with the intention of not returning to it could constitute the case of apostasy from his religious institute. In the case of one who is lawfully away from his religious house for a long time, *e. g.*, the parochial vicar, it is only when he has withdrawn from obedience to his superiors for more than a month that he would have to be considered an apostate.[41] A religious who is authorized by indult to be temporarily absent from his religious house, but who has been dismissed by a bishop upon a three years' experiment, is under obligation in virtue of his continuing religious vows to return to his religious institute, and his superiors have a corresponding duty to seek him and to receive him into a house of the institute. If he does not return he may be compared to an apostate or at least to a fugitive, but in practice the strict consequences of these concepts cannot always be urged, for reasons may exist either on the part of the religious or on the part of the institute to nullify the legal force of these demands.[42]

It has been stated that the religious in order to be guilty of the crime of apostasy from his institute must unlawfully, *i. e.*, without permission, leave his religious house or the place to which he has been assigned in obedience. It is therefore necessary to consider the various kinds of permission. The authors treat these in connection with the vow of poverty, but the concepts apply also to the case in which permission is given to leave the religious house.

A permission to be effective must have certain qualities. It must be *free, i. e.*, not extorted by fraud, deceit, force or fear; and *legiti-*

[39] Canons 465, §§ 4, 5; 475; 476.

[40] Coronata, *Institutiones*, n. 642.

[41] Augustine, *A Commentary on the New Code of Canon Law* (8 vols., Vol. VIII, 2. ed., St. Louis: Herder, 1924), VIII, p. 472, note. 1.

[42] Larraona, "Studia Canonica,"—*CpR*, XII (1931), 61; cf. *infra*, pp. 122, 123.

mate, i. e., granted by a competent superior. A legitimate permission is *valid,* when it is within the power of the superior to grant it; *licit,* when it is given for a sufficient reason.[43]

As to its extent a permission is either general or particular. From the viewpoint of the number of persons concerned a permission is *general* when it is given to many, *particular* when it is given to one individual. From the viewpoint of the number of cases comprehended a *general* permission is one which is given for a number of cases, a *particular* permission is one which is given for a single instance.[44]

As to its form a permission is *express* if the consent of the superior is given in words or signs. It is *implicit* when it is contained indirectly in an act or situation that is expressly permitted. It is *tacit* if it results from the silence of the superior when the superior knows of the matter of the permission and is free to manifest his dissent. A reasonably *presumed* permission is one based on a prudent judgment that the superior would grant the permission if asked. There are two requisites for the licit use of a presumed permission: first, that the superior cannot be approached without grave inconvenience, and secondly, that there is at least a moral need to act.[45]

The permission which a religious needs in order to leave his religious house must therefore be a permission which is given freely and legitimately. If the permission is extorted by fraud, deceit, fear or force it is not free and is therefore invalid.[46] A religious who proposes but a false reason when he seeks permission to leave the

[43] Schaefer, *De Religiosis,* n. 330; Turner, *The Vow of Poverty,* The Catholic University of America Canon Law Studies, n. 54 (Washington, D. C.: The Catholic University of America, 1929), p. 102.

[44] Aertnys-Damen, *Theologia Moralis* (13. ed., 2 vols., Taurini, Romae: Marietti, 1939), I, n. 1210.

[45] Turner, *op. cit.,* pp. 103, 104. Sometimes the fact that the superior would grant the permission if he were asked is put down as one of the conditions. The judgment that the superior is willing is of the very essence of a presumed permission; it is merely a condition for its use.

[46] Schaefer, *De Religiosis,* n. 330.

house is by his act of departure unlawfully outside of his religious house, for the apparently obtained permission is invalid.[47]

The permission to leave one's religious house must also be legitimate. The permission must be granted by a competent superior and must be given according to the law and the constitutions of the institute. The powers of superiors to grant permission to leave the house are restricted by canon law.[48] Thus a superioress of nuns (*moniales*) cannot grant permission to leave the religious house, except in the case of imminent danger of death or of very grave impending harm.[49] The power of other superiors is limited by the character of the institute, in accordance with its furthering of the active or of the contemplative life, and by the character of the religious who wishes to leave the house, in accordance with the duties which he has as an official of the house, or as one having the care of souls, etc.[50] Here it may be noted that a superior is an apostate from his religious institute if he exceeds the limits of canon law and his constitutions in leaving his religious house and has the necessary intention of perpetually deserting the institute.

One must voluntarily leave his religious house before he can be classed as an apostate. If he is forced to leave, as in the case of a dismissed religious, he is not an apostate, unless he committed the crime for the purpose of being dismissed, in which case he is an apostate.[51]

The leaving of the house must in its intent be deliberate. To be deliberate the intention must be based on full knowledge and com-

[47] Goyeneche, "Consultationes,"—*CpR,* XVII (1936), 345-347. Schaefer, when speaking of the requisites for a permission, admits that a permission obtained by fraud or deceit is invalid (*De Religiosis,* n. 330); but, when speaking of a religious who leaves his house under a fraudulently obtained permission, he says that the religious is not a fugitive in the juridic sense if he leaves with an invalid permission (*ibid.,* n. 567). He also cites the contrary opinion of Goyeneche.

[48] Canons 601, 606, 607.

[49] Canon 601.

[50] Oesterle, "Casus in Canonem 2385,"—*Apollinaris,* X (1937), 124-132.

[51] Schmalzgrueber, Lib. V, tit. IX, n. 14; Piatus Montensis, *Praelectiones Juris Regularis,* I, q. 216, 4; Vermeersch, *De Religiosis Institutis et Personis,* I, n. 341.

plete freedom of will. Any circumstance which reacts upon these two requisites will correspondingly take away, increase or diminish the imputability of the crime of apostasy.[52] The religious must actually leave the house otherwise he does not commit the crime of apostasy from his religious institute. As has been stated, when a lawfully absent religious deserts the place assigned to him by obedience and forms the intention of removing himself from obedience to his superiors, he is from that moment unlawfully outside of his religious house, and becomes an apostate from his institute.[53]

The religious house is to be taken in its widest sense, including all the buildings which the religious inhabit, together with the property of the religious. The religious house, relative to apostasy or flight, is not restricted to the limits of the cloister.[54]

The older authors disputed the point as to how great a distance from the religious house one had to go before becoming an apostate or fugitive. Some demanded a distance sufficiently great in itself to imply the commission of a mortal sin. The better opinion seems to be that the religious is an apostate as soon as he sets foot outside of his religious house with the intention of not returning to the institute. The reason is that the gravity of these crimes is measured not from the actual leaving of the house, but by the intention with which the religious leaves, namely, the intention of deserting his institute for a time in the case of a fugitive, or permanently in the case of an apostate.[55] One is therefore an apostate from the first moment that he is outside of his religious house when he is motivated with the intention of deserting his institute, *i. e.*, as soon as the elements of the crime are present.[56] This opinion is based on the

[52] Canons 2199-2207.

[53] *Supra*, p. 57.

[54] Oesterle, *loc. cit.;* Piatus Montensis, *Praelectiones Juris Regularis,* I, q. 216, 3; Rotarius, *Theologia Moralis Regularium* (3 tomes in 2, Venetiis, 1735), Tom. I, lib. III, c. I, punct. III, n. 1; Matthaeucci, *Officialis Curiae Regularis,* I, p. 61, nn. 8, 9, 10.

[55] Piatus Montensis, *op. cit.,* I, qq. 216, 513; Rotarius, *op. cit.,* Tom. I, lib. III, c. I, punct. IV, n. 7; Passerinus, *De Hominum Statibus et Officiis Inspectiones Morales* (3 vols., Lucae, 1732), Q. CLXXX, art. VIII, n. 253.

[56] Passerinus, *loc. cit.;* Rotarius, *loc. cit.;* Vermeersch-Creusen, *Epitome,* III, n. 589.

decree of Clement VIII in which he stated that apostasy is reserved "*quando eo pervenerit ut extra septa monasterii, seu conventus, egressio fiat.*" [57]

B. The Intention: The Non-Return or the Removal of Oneself From Religious Obedience

1. The Intention

The act of apostasy from religion is a mixed act, composed of the external element—the unlawful departure from one's religious house, and the internal element—the intention of not returning to the religious institute. The intention is the principal element,[58] since by the intention apostasy is formally distinguished from flight. The intention, because it is something internal, must be manifested externally, for it is necessary that the specific note of apostasy be externally apparent.[59] Unlawful departure from one's religious house is not of itself a manifestation of the intention of not returning. The intention of not returning must be externalized by words, signs or actions.[60] In the absence of such signs the law admits of presumptions based on external facts.[61] This external manifestation of intention, or the justified presumption of its existence, is necessary if the religious is to be considered an apostate in the external forum.[62]

Finally, the intention must be criminal, *i. e.*, it must be of the character which is presupposed for constituting the crime of apostasy from one's religious institute. That intention consists in the desire of perpetually deserting one's religious institute. The Code speaks of two possible intentions: the one of not returning, in the case of a

[57] Clement VIII, decr. *Sanctissumus,* 26 maii 1593, § 1, n. 2—*Fontes,* n. 177; Bizzarri, pp. 274, 275.

[58] Blat, *Ius de Religiosis,* n. 649; Piatus Montensis, *Praelectiones Juris Regularis,* I, q. 225; Rotarius, *Theologia Moralis Regularium,* Tom. I, lib. III, c. I, punct. IV, n. 4; Vermeersch-Creusen, *Epitome,* III, n. 589.

[59] Vermeersch-Creusen, *loc. cit.*

[60] Goyeneche, *De Religiosis,* n. 102; De Meester, *Compendium,* n. 1888.

[61] Canon 644, § 2; cf. *infra,* p. 67.

[62] Goyeneche, "Consultationes,"—*CpR,* IX (1928), 427-433; *idem., De Religiosis,* n. 102; Schaefer, *De Religiosis,* n. 571.

religious who unlawfully leaves his religious house, and the other, of removing oneself from religious obedience, in the case of a religious who has lawfully left the house.[63] These two intentions mean the same thing—deserting one's religious institute.[64]

Schmalzgrueber indicated a third possible class of apostates when he spoke of "a religious who leaves without the intention of returning".[65] It seems that such an absence of an intention of returning to the religious institute is easily reducible to an implicit intention of not returning to it. When a religious obtains permission to go out, it is understood that he is not permitted to stay out indefinitely.[66] A religious must have a habitual intention of returning. If the religious in leaving the house excludes this habitual intention of returning, he therefore has an implicit intention of not returning, which is sufficient for the crime. This implicit intention is found in the explicit exclusion of his habitual intention to return. It is not necessary that there be an oral or a mental exclusion of the habitual intention. The exclusion may be found *in actu exercito, e. g.*, a religious packs his trunk, etc., and does not even give a thought to the intention of returning or of not returning, but his intention is bound up with the very act he does.[67]

A question arises relative to a religious who leaves with a conditional intention of not returning. If the religious has not left the house, but has the intention of leaving permanently if a certain condition is fulfilled, he is not an apostate, since an actual leaving of the house is required. Moreover, in the case in which the religious has already left the house and has the intention of not returning if a certain condition is fulfilled, *e. g.*, if the Superior is reappointed, if

[63] Canon 644, § 1.

[64] Schaefer, *De Religiosis*, n. 565; Beste, *Introductio in Codicem*, p. 437.

[65] Lib. V, tit. IX, n. 11. Reiffenstuel (Lib. III, tit. XXXI, n. 251) stated that the formal cause of apostasy consisted in this alone that the religious in deserting the religious institute did so "without the intention of returning."

[66] Woywod, "Apostasy from Religious Life,"—*The Homiletic and Pastoral Review*, XXXIX (1938-1939), 265-274 (hereafter to be cited as *HPR*).

[67] Rotarius, *Theologia Moralis Regularium*, Tom. I, lib. III, c. I, punct. IV, n. 3. Intentio actualis elici potest vel *in actu—signato,* quando elicitur expresse ore vel mente; vel *in actu exercito,* quando quis opus facit sciens et advertens quid faciat.—Aertyns-Damen, *Theologia Moralis,* II, 10, nota 1.

his mother dies, etc., such a religious cannot be considered to have the intention of deserting his institute since his intention is *de futuro* and depends on a future fact.[68] Since the religious has not the absolute intention of deserting his religious institute and since his habitual intention of returning endures for the present inasmuch as its revocation is conditioned on a future fact, he is a fugitive if he unlawfully leaves or is already outside of his religious house; but when the fact upon which his conditional intention depends is realized he becomes either an apostate or simply remains a fugitive in accordance with the nature of his intention from that moment onward.

The intention which the religious must necessarily be presupposed to have before he becomes an apostate is the intention of not returning to his religious *institute.* The religious who leaves his religious house with the intention of not returning to *that house,* but who has not the intention of deserting the institute, is not an apostate.[69] He must have the intention of perpetually deserting the institute.[70] But in non-centralized institutes a religious who deserts his monastery *(sui iuris)* with the intention of not returning to it is an apostate, if he made his profession for that house.[71]

A religious is not an apostate when without permission he leaves his religious house to go directly to the Holy See, or to go to his major superiors to seek redress for unjust treatment by a lesser superior.[72] In this case the religious may be said to appeal because

[68] Cf. Goyeneche, "Consultationes,"—*CpR,* VII (1926), 252-254.

[69] Schaefer, *De Religiosis,* n. 565; Coronata, *Institutiones,* n. 642; Beste, *Introductio in Codicem,* p. 437; Wernz-Vidal, *Ius Canonicum,* III, n. 431; Pejska, *Jus Canonicum Religiosorum,* p. 188; Berutti, *De Religiosis,* n. 156.

[70] Schmalzgrueber, Lib. III, tit. XXXI, n. 266; Reiffenstuel, Lib. III, tit. XXXI, n. 251; Piatus Montensis, *Praelectiones Juris Regularis,* I, q. 215; De Meester, *Compendium,* n. 1054.

[71] Coronata, *Institutiones,* n. 2188; Augustine, *A Commentary,* VIII, 468, 469.

[72] Benedict XIV, *De Synodo Dioecesana,* Lib. XIII, c. IX, n. 14; Schmalzgrueber, Lib. V, tit. IX, n. 16; Ferraris, *Prompta Bibliotheca,* s. v. "Apostasia," nn. 30, 31; Schaefer, *De Religiosis,* n. 566; Coronata, *Institutiones,* n. 642; Augustine, *A Commentary on the New Code of Canon Law* (8 vols., Vol. III, 4. ed., St. Louis: Herder, 1929), III, 382.

of injustice. To defend oneself against an injustice is a right based on the law of nature. There is no reason why a religious because of his state should be in an inferior condition to another man.[73] The chief reason why the religious is not an apostate is that he has not the intention of deserting his religious institute. Moreover, if the religious cannot get permission from his immediate superior to go to a higher superior, can he not presume the permission of his higher superior to go to him, if this is not forbidden by the constitutions of his institute? In this case he would not be illegitimately outside of his house.[74]

The question arises whether a religious is an apostate if he unlawfully and without a rescript of the Holy See leaves his religious house to transfer to another religious institute. The authors who wrote before the Code disputed whether such a religious was an apostate as long as there was no statement in the constitutions of his religious institute to indicate that he incurred the penalties for apostasy. Suarez,[75] Rotarius [76] and Castropalao [77] claimed that such a religious was an apostate. The common opinion [78] was that he was not an apostate, since he did not have the intention of deserting the religious state but only his particular religious institute.[79] Of the authors who wrote after the Code the greater number stated that a religious who leaves his institute without an apostolic indult and goes

[73] Ferraris, *loc. cit.*

[74] Esswein, *The Extrajudicial Coercive Powers of Ecclesiastical Superiors,* The Catholic University of America Canon Law Studies, n. 127 (Washington, D. C.: The Catholic University of America Press, 1941), p. 88.

[75] Tr. VIII, lib. III, c. XII, n. 17.

[76] Tom. I, lib. III, c. I, punct. IV, n. 8.

[77] *Opus Morale* (2 vols., Venetiis, 1702), Tr. XVI, disp. IV, punct. XVI, n. 7.

[78] Cf. Castropalao, *op. cit.,* n. 6; Piatus Montensis, *Praelectiones Juris Regularis,* I, q. 218.

[79] Reiffenstuel, Lib. V, tit. IX, n. 13; Passerinus, *De Hominum Statibus et Officiis Inspectiones Morales,* Q. CLXXXIX, art. VIII, n. 133; Vermeersch, *De Religiosis Institutis et Personis,* I, n. 341; Van Hove, "Apostasy,"—*The Catholic Encyclopedia* (17 vols. and 2 supplements, New York: The Encyclopedia Press, 1906-1922), I, 625.

to another religious institute is an apostate.[80] Voltas says that the opinion which denies that such religious are apostates because they do not desert the religious state [81] is improbable.[82] When one by religious profession enters the religious state he does not enter it *in abstracto,* but he enters it as a certain kind of religious, *e. g.*, as a Redemptorist, a Dominican.[83] He who unlawfully deserts his institute, thereby unlawfully deserts the religious state. It cannot be claimed that he immediately enters another institute, since such an entry is invalid without an apostolic indult. Besides, canon 644, § 1, seems to decide the problem. The religious is unlawfully outside of his religious institute with the intention of not returning. Once these factors are verified it seems to be altogether immaterial and irrelevant if one can incidentally point to the presence of a desire to join another institute.

If a religious flees to the house of another institute to have recourse to the Holy See or to his own major superiors he is not an apostate, for he has no intention of removing himself from the obedience which is due to his own superior.[84]

2. *The Presumption*

As has already been stated, the intention of not returning to the religious institute must be manifested externally if the religious is to be considered an apostate in the external forum.[85] This manifestation can be by signs, words, actions or circumstances. Such manifestations of a malicious intention of not returning are present: if the religious commits one of the three crimes punished with automatic

[80] Coronata, *Institutiones,* I, p. 861, n. 642, nota 7; Wernz-Vidal, *Ius Canonicum,* III, p. 466, n. 431, nota 28; Schaefer, *De Religiosis,* n. 566; Berutti, *De Religiosis,* n. 156; Augustine, *A Commentary,* III, 382; Voltas, "Consultationes,"—*CpR,* I (1920), 271, nota 1.

[81] De Siena, *Commentarium Censurarum iuxta Novum Codicem Iuris Canonici,* (Neapoli, 1918), p. 584; Sole, *De Delictis et Poenis* (Romae: Pustet, 1920), n. 445; Biederlack-Führich, *De Religiosis,* n. 169.

[82] Voltas, *loc. cit.*

[83] Goyeneche, "De Transitu ad aliam Religionem,"—*CpR,* I (1920), 218.

[84] Coronata, *Institutiones,* n. 642; Wernz-Vidal, *Ius Canonicum,* III, p. 466, n. 431, nota 28.

[85] *Supra,* p. 62.

dismissal in canon 646, namely, apostasy from the faith, flight with a person of the other sex, and the contracting or the attempt of contracting marriage, or if the religious takes a long journey, or if he undertakes some employment incompatible with the religious state, or if he packs up the various articles which he has for his personal use in indication of an indefinite absence, or if he tells someone, or leaves a note in which he reveals his intention of not returning.[86] When such evidences are present the religious may be immediately presumed to be an apostate from his institute. However, before the lapse of a month the burden of proof of a malicious intention is on the institute, and the religious does not have to prove that he did not have the malicious intention. Putting off the religious habit was a sign of the intention of not returning under the law before the Code in view of the *latae sententiae* excommunication enacted in the common law for putting off the habit.[87] Under the present law putting off the habit no longer is recognized as constituting a certain sign; rather it induces a grave suspicion of the intention of not returning.[88]

In the absence of any evidences of an intention of not returning to the religious institute the law establishes a presumption. It states that the malicious intention is presumed if the religious within a month neither returns nor manifests to his superior his intention of returning.[89]

Since the religious becomes an apostate from his religious institute the moment he deserts his religious house or the place assigned to him by obedience,[90] the starting point for the computation of the month's absence is implicitly determined. Therefore, the month is computed according to canon 34, § 3. Thus, in the case of a religious who has unlawfully left, according to canon 34, § 3, n. 1, the month is taken

[86] Wernz-Vidal, *Ius Canonicum*, III, n. 431; Pejska, *Ius Canonicum Religiosorum*, p. 187; Chelodi-Dalpiaz, *Ius Poenale*, n. 101; Beste, *Introductio in Codicem*, p. 437; Vermeersch-Creusen, *Epitome*, III, n. 589; Schaefer, *De Religiosis*, n. 571; Berutti, *De Religiosis*, n. 156.

[87] C. 2, *ne clerici vel monachi saecularibus negotiis se immisceant*, III, 24, in VI°.

[88] Vermeersch-Creusen, *Epitome*, III, n. 589.

[89] Canon 644, § 2.

[90] *Supra*, pp. 61, 62.

as in the calendar, and according to n. 3 the day on which he leaves is not counted and the month is completed with the end of the last day which bears the same numerical date. In the case of a religious who is lawfully outside of his religious house the time is computed from the time when he should have returned. Thus if the religious was to return at a specified time on a given day, according to canon 34, § 3, n. 1, the month is taken as in the calendar, and according to n. 3 the day on which he should have returned is not counted and the month is completed with the end of the last day which bears the same numerical date. If no specific time of day was set for the return of the religious, he could have returned at any time during that day. In this case according to canon 34, § 3, n. 1, the month is taken as in the calendar, and according to n. 2, the month begins with the midnight following the day on which he should have returned and is completed at the beginning of the day which bears the same numerical date on which the month began to lapse.

This presumption of a malicious intention of not returning gives the religious institute grounds on which to act. Even though the intention is not manifested externally, yet after the month the religious can be considered an apostate in the external forum, and punished as such.[91] The presumption is a *praesumptio iuris tantum* [92] and admits of both direct and indirect proof to the contrary.[93]

As the overthrowing of this presumption is a matter belonging to the external forum the religious must prove in some external way [94] that he was not unlawfully absent for a month, or that he did not have the intention of deserting the institute, or that because of circumstances, *e. g.*, war, pestilence, etc., he could not notify his superior of his intention of returning.[95] This he can prove by means of the

[91] Cocchi, *De Delictis et Poenis*, n. 261; Goyeneche, "Consultationes,"—*CpR*, VII (1926), 252-254.

[92] Vermeersch-Creusen, *Epitome*, III, n. 746; Schaefer, *De Religiosis*, n. 565; Augustine, *A Commentary*, III, 382; Cappello, *De Censuris*, n. 390.

[93] Canon 1826. Direct proof overthrows the presumption itself, indirect proof overthrows the fact on which the presumption is based. Thus the proving that the religious was not absent for a month is indirect proof; all other proof constitutes direct proof.

[94] Goyeneche, "Consultationes,"—*CpR*, VII (1926), 252-254.

[95] Schaefer, *loc. cit.*, Berutti, *De Religiosis*, n. 156.

adjuncts and circumstances of his departure, and of the things that happened before, during and after his absence from the institute.[96] An explicit manifestation of his intention to return does not seem necessary. Thus, if one who is illegitimately absent corresponds with his superior there seems to be an implicit intention of returning which is sufficiently externalized to overthrow the presumption of an intention of not returning.[97] Augustine says that the presumption against the religious ceases if the religious can prove by one trustworthy witness that he wrote to his superior.[98]

Once the presumption has been established, it stands until it is peremptorily overthrown. The presumption is not weakened by a presumption of ignorance, since ignorance or error in regard to a law or penalty is generally not presumed.[99] If affected, crass or supine ignorance is proved it does not excuse from any of the penalties. Gravely culpable ignorance, however, excuses from the excommunication, but not from the vindicative penalties.[100]

[96] Oesterle, "Casus in Canonem 2385,"—*Apollinaris,* X (1927), 127.

[97] Coronata, *Institutiones,* n. 642.

[98] *A Commentary,* III, 382.

[99] Canon 16, § 2.

[100] Canon 2229, §§ 1, 3, n. 1.

CHAPTER VIII

FUGITIVES FROM RELIGIOUS INSTITUTES

Canon 644, § 3. Fugitivus est qui, sine Superiorum licentia, domum religiosam deserit cum animo ad religionem redeundi.[1]

Since religious are bound by reason of their state to persevere in it until death,[2] the Church punishes as a crime even the temporary desertion of one's religious institute. The fugitive commits a crime which is constituted by two elements, namely, the *fact* of the unlawful departure from the religious house, and the *intention* of returning to the institute.

A. The Fact: Unlawful Departure From the Religious House

1. The Profession

Unlike the definition of an apostate, the definition of a fugitive makes no mention of vows. Therefore it makes no difference if a religious who deserts his religious house with the intention of returning to the institute has temporary vows, or solemn vows, or simple perpetual vows.[3] Schaefer says that even novices can be fugitives, but that they cannot be bound to the penalties, since canon 2386 speaks of "fugitive religious".[4] To include a novice within the definition of a fugitive seems to extend the term "fugitive" beyond its

[1] Canon 644, § 3. A fugitive is one who, without the permission of his superiors, deserts the religious house but with the intention of returning to the institute. (Authorized English Translation.)

[2] *Supra*, p. 3.

[3] Coronata, *Institutiones*, n. 642; Schaefer, *De Religiosis*, n. 567; Goyeneche, *De Religiosis*, n. 102; Chelodi-Dalpiaz, *Ius Poenale*, n. 101; Berutti, *De Religiosis*, n. 156.

[4] Schaefer, *loc. cit.*

intended meaning, for a novice is juridically free to leave at any time,[5] and no one would consider the superior to be in any way bound to seek and receive back a novice who unlawfully leaves the novitiate. Moreover, Title XV of Book II of the Code treats of religious who leave the institute. Novices are not religious in the strict sense. Novices cannot therefore be fugitives.[6] An exception to this general rule would be had in the case of a professed religious who has transferred to another institute, and unlawfully leaves the novitiate of the second institute with the intention of returning after a time to the institute in which he is professed. Such a religious is unlawfully outside the place assigned to him by obedience and has the intention of temporarily deserting the institute in which he is professed. He is, therefore a fugitive.

As has been stated,[7] since canon 681 applies canon 645 *"congrua congruis referendo"*, the notions of an apostate and also of a fugitive are applicable to members of societies living in common without vows. It was stated that these cannot be apostates in the strict sense since they have no vows; but since there is no mention of vows in the definition of a fugitive they can be fugitives in the strict sense.[8] However, with respect to the application of the penalties there is some dispute in regard to non-clerical societies.[9]

Women religious can also be fugitives, since there is no exclusion of them in the law.[10] They cannot incur the penalty of suspension, but they can incur the other penalties.

Servants and others who are not members of the institute, and who live in a house of clerical religious and are according to canon 514, § 1, subject to the superior of the house, cannot come within the notion of fugitives if they leave with the intention of returning, since they always retain their juridical liberty to go as they please.

[5] Canon 571, § 1.

[6] Cappello, *De Censuris*, n. 538; Chelodi-Dalpiaz, *Ius Poenale*, n. 101; Berutti, *De Religiosis*, n. 156.

[7] *Supra*, p. 54.

[8] Coronata, *Institutiones*, n. 642; Schaefer, *De Religiosis*, n. 467; Goyeneche, *De Religiosis*, n. 102.

[9] *Infra*, pp. 101, 102.

[10] *Supra*, p. 53.

2. *The Egress*

To be a fugitive the religious [11] must unlawfully leave his religious house. The phrase "leaves his religious house" is, as with apostasy, not to be taken strictly. The religious who unlawfully leaves his house to go to another house of the institute is not a fugitive, for he does not desert his institute.[12] A religious is a fugitive if he lawfully leaves his religious house but stays outside one of the houses of his institute beyond the time fixed by the superior, or if he deserts the place assigned through obedience, since he is from that moment unlawfully outside his religious house.[13] An example of this would obtain in the case of a missionary who after a mission does not return to one of the houses of his institute, but without any kind of permission of his superior stays in a place other than a house of his institute. Likewise, the case would obtain when a religious who is sent by his superior to another house of the institute on business or for relaxation, would instead stay in a place other than a house of his institute, and do this without any kind of permission from his superior. It must be remarked that if his action is covered by at least a reasonably presumed permission of his superior he is not unlawfully outside his religious house and is not a fugitive.

What has been said with regard to apostates relative to the qualities of the permission, the kinds of permission and the incurring of the penalties at the moment the religious leaves the house [14] holds with equal force in regard to fugitives.

The religious must actually be outside of his religious house to be a fugitive. The intention alone of deserting the institute temporarily is not sufficient. The crime of flight must be externalized before it can come under the external forum.[15]

[11] Whenever the term religious is used in connection with flight from an institute it will be understood to refer also to the members of societies who live in common without vows unless the contrary is indicated.

[12] *Infra*, pp. 74, 75.

[13] Schaefer, *De Religiosis*, n. 567; Beste, *Introductio in Codicem*, p. 437.

[14] *Supra*, pp. 58-60.

[15] Cappello, *De Censuris*, n. 538.

B. The Intention: Temporary Desertion of the Institute and the Return to It

1. *The Intention*

The intention with which the fugitive leaves, namely, the intention of deserting the institute for a time and of then returning to it, formally distinguishes the crime of the fugitive from that of the apostate.[16] This intention must be manifested externally in order that his action can be recognized as the specific crime of flight and made punishable as a crime.[17]

The essential difference between the intention of the apostate and that of the fugitive is that the apostate intends to desert the institute perpetually, the fugitive only for a time.[18] Some of the authors say that the fugitive deserts the religious house and not the institute.[19] Schaefer [20] and De Meester [21] admit with many other authors [22] that the fugitive intends to remove himself from religious obedience for a time. As has been said with reference to the two ways of becoming an apostate as stated in canon 644, § 1, the phrase "removing oneself from religious obedience" means the same as deserting the institute.[23] Now if anyone removes himself from obedience tem-

[16] Wernz, *Ius Decretalium,* III, n. 675; Piatus Montensis, *Praelectiones Juris Regularis,* I. q. 225; Vermeersch-Creusen, *Epitome,* III, n. 589; Goyeneche, "Consultationes,"—*CpR,* XVIII (1936), 345-347.

[17] Canon 2195; cf. Cocchi, *De Delictis et Poenis,* n. 262; Beste, *Introductio in Codicem,* p. 968.

[18] Wernz, *loc. cit.;* Fanfani, *De Iure Religiosorum,* n. 491.

[19] Schaefer, *De Religiosis,* n. 567, De Meester, *Compendium,* n. 1055; Cocchi, *De Religiosis et Laicis,* n. 140.

[20] *Loc cit.*

[21] *Op. cit.,* n. 1889.

[22] Suarez, Tr. VIII, lib. III, c. II, n. 10; Reiffenstuel, Lib. III, tit. XXXI, n. 251; Schmalzgrueber, Lib. III, tit. XXXI, n. 266; Piatus Montensis, *Praelectiones Juris Regularis,* I, q. 225; Rotarius, *Theologia Moralis Regularium,* Tom. I, lib. III, c. I, punct. III, n. 1, 2; Vermeersch, *De Religiosis Institutis et Personis,* I, n. 340; Wernz, *loc. cit.;* Coronata, *Institutiones,* n. 642; Blat, *Ius de Religiosis,* n. 649; Pruemmer, *Manuale Iuris Canonici,* q. 256; Ayrinhac-Lydon, *Penal Legislation,* pp. 299, 300; Augustine, *A Commentary,* III, 383; Beste, *Introductio in Codicem,* p. 437; Papi, *Religious in Church Law,* p. 8.

[23] *Supra,* pp. 62, 63.

porarily it is the equivalent of deserting the institute temporarily. Canon 644, § 3, states that the fugitive leaves with the intention of returning to the institute (*ad religionem*). Moreover, canon 645, § 1, in speaking of the obligation of the fugitive to return, states that he must return to the institute (*ad religionem*). Schaefer in admitting this adds that he need not have the intention of returning to the same house, and he also admits that one who deserts his house in order to go to another of the same institute, or in order to approach his major superiors or the Holy See, is not a fugitive.[24] Another argument may be drawn from the wording of the title in the Code under which the definition of a fugitive is given. The heading is titled: "Egress from the Religious Institute." Schmalzgrueber expressly states that a fugitive deserts his institute.[25]

The religious who deserts his religious house and goes to another house of his institute, or who goes to his major superiors or to the Holy See to seek redress because of some vexation from his local superior does not desert the institute and hence is not a fugitive.[26] Coronata says that a religious who without permission leaves his religious house under the pretext of going to his superiors or to the Holy See can be considered a fugitive unless he can prove that he asked permission and that it was unjustly denied him. Then he says that one is not a fugitive if, to free himself from the vexations of his local superior, he deserts the house and goes directly to another house of the institute.[27] Now, if a religious goes to his major superior he is ordinarily going to another house of the institute. Or if perhaps the major superior is outside of any of the houses of the institute the religious can reasonably presume his permission to come to him, unless the religious is forbidden by the constitutions to make such an approach without written permission. Moreover, in the in-

[24] *Loc. cit.*

[25] Lib. III, tit. XXXI, n. 266.

[26] Schaefer, *De Religiosis*, n. 567; Fanfani, *De Iure Religiosorum*, n. 491; Blat, *Ius de Religiosis*, n. 649; Goyeneche, *De Religiosis*, n. 102; Toso, *Commentaria Minora*, Lib. II, pars I, tom. III, p. 240; Wernz-Vidal, *Ius Canonicum*, III, n. 432; Coronata, *Institutiones*, n. 642; Augustine, *A Commentary*, III, 383; Berutti, *De Religiosis*, n. 156.

[27] *Institutiones*, n. 642, 2.

terpretation given to the canon of the Council of Trent which forbade regulars to leave their convents on the pretext of going to their superiors [28] the word *pretext* was understood to mean a light cause or no cause at all.[29]

To be a fugitive, and not an apostate, the religious in unlawfully leaving his religious house must have the intention of returning to the institute, even though he does not intend to return to the same house from which he left.[30] This intention need not be express. It is sufficiently contained in the external manifestation of the intention of remaining away *for but a time.*

If the religious remains away even over a month, but has the intention of returning, he is but a fugitive and not an apostate.[31] He would, however, have to prove that he had had the intention of returning in order to overthrow the presumption of canon 644, § 2, which states that after a month's unlawful absence a religious is presumed to be an apostate.

2. *The Time Element*

The fugitive intends to desert the institute *for a time.* Though the *latae sententiae* penalties are contracted as soon as the religious leaves his religious house, the Code does not state how long he must intend to stay away in order to be considered a fugitive. The authors usually say that the intention of an absence of two or three days is required before the religious can be considered a fugitive.[32]

[28] Conc. Trident., sess. XXV, *de regularibus,* c. 4.

[29] Benedictus XIV, *De Synodo Dioecesana,* Lib. XIII, c. XI, n. 14; Ferraris, *Prompta Bibliotheca,* s. v. "Apostasia," n. 32.

[30] Canon 645, § 1; cf., Schaefer, *De Religiosis,* n. 567; Berutti, *De Religiosis,* n. 156.

[31] Coronata, *Institutiones,* n. 642; Goyeneche, "Consultationes,"—*CpR,* VII (1926), 252-254.

[32] Schaefer, *De Religiosis,* n. 567; Vermeersch-Creusen, *Epitome,* I, n. 746; III, n. 590; Chelodi, *Ius de Personis,* p. 450, n. 288, nota 3; Cocchi, *De Delictis et Poenis,* n. 262; Ayrinhac-Lydon, *Penal Legislation,* p. 300; Beste, *Introductio in Codicem,* p. 437; Wernz-Vidal, *Ius Canonicum,* III, n. 432; Woywod, "Apostasy from Religious Life,"—*HPR,* XXXIX (1938-1939), 270; Goyeneche, *De Religiosis,* p. 202, note 45.

Goyeneche says that if a religious legitimately goes out and protracts his stay beyond the time fixed by his permission, he must intend to be away three or more days before he can be considered a fugitive.[33]

When it comes to the application of the penalties, inasmuch as the authors speak of two or three days, three days must be supposed as necessary, for in the application of penalties a strict interpretation is to be employed.[34]

All the authors admit that a lesser time than two days is not sufficient to constitute one a fugitive. Such a shorter time, rather constitutes an illicit or furtive egress,[35] for the religious in this case does not intend to *desert* the institute or to remove himself from religious obedience.[36]

In regard to furtive egress a comparison with the doctrine of theologians on sin may be instituted. The theologians say that both mortal and venial sin is an offense against God, but the sinner who commits mortal sin turns away from God, whereas the sinner who commits venial sin merely turns to creatures. So in flight the fugitive deserts the institute, but the religious by furtive egress merely commits an act of disobedience.

The authors limit the time of furtive egress to a short time, whether for some hours or for a whole day. Berutti alone speaks of one or the other day.[37] As has been stated, the authors require a two or three days' absence for one to be a fugitive and for the ap-

[33] Goyeneche, *loc. cit.; idem.*, "Consultationes,"—*CpR,* XVII (1936), 345, 346.

[34] Canon 19; Reg. 15, R. J., in VI°.

[35] Canon 606, § 1.

[36] Suarez, Tr. VIII, lib. III, c. I, n. 1; Rotarius, *Theologia Moralis Regularium,* Tom. I, lib. III, c. I, punct. III, nn. 1, 2; Piatus Montensis, *Praelectiones Juris Regularis,* I, q. 225; Wernz, *Ius Decretalium,* III, n. 675; Vermeersch, *De Religiosis Institutis et Personis,* I, n. 340; Vermeersch-Creusen, *Epitome,* I, n. 746; III, n. 590; Pruemmer, *Manuale Iuris Canonici,* q. 256; Coronata, *Institutiones,* n. 642; Goyeneche, *De Religiosis,* n. 102; *idem.*, "Consultationes,"—*CpR,* XVII (1936), 345-347; Toso, *Commentaria Minora,* Lib. II, pars I, tom. III, p. 241; Beste, *Introductio in Codicem,* p. 437; Ayrinhac-Lydon, *Penal Legislation,* pp. 299, 300; Woywod, "Apostasy from Religious Life,"—*HPR,* XXXIX (1938-1939), 266; Berutti, *De Religiosis,* n. 156.

[37] *Loc. cit.*

plication of the penalties three days are required.[38] It seems, therefore, that the time which connotes nothing more than a furtive egress can be extended to two days.

In the Order of Preachers (Dominicans) one night's absence without permission begets the presumption that the religious is a fugitive.[39] The constitutions of the Discalced Trinitarians state that whosoever goes out of the convent at night, or stays outside of the convent for eight days is subject to the penalties of fugitives.[40] The constitutions of the Friars Minor indicate the penalties of canon 2385 for apostasy and state that one is an *apostate* if he is unlawfully outside the monastery for a natural day.[41] Thus a Franciscan incurs the same penalties that the Code inflicts on apostates, but he incurs them by particular law. It must be noted that if he leaves with the intention of not returning, he is an apostate according to the Code and incurs the penalties by reason of the Code from the moment he leaves.

What has been stated in regard to the computation of time with regard to apostates[42] holds also for the computation of time in connection with a fugitive, unless the constitutions state otherwise.

[38] *Supra*, pp. 75, 76.

[39] *Constitutiones Fratrum Sacri Ordinis Praedicatorum* (Romae, 1933), const. 197, §§ II, IV.

[40] *Regula Primitiva et Constitutiones Fratrum Discalceatorum Ordinis Sanctissimae Trinitatis Redemptionis Captivorum* (Isola del Lira: Soc. Tip. A. Macioce & Pisani, 1933), const. 245.

[41] *The Rule and General Constitutions of the Friars Minor* (Paterson, N. J., 1936), n. 126.

[42] *Supra*, pp. 67, 68.

CHAPTER IX

THE PENALTIES INCURRED BY APOSTATES FROM RELIGIOUS INSTITUTES

Canon 2385. Firmo praescripto canon 646, religiosus apostata a religione, ipso iure incurrit in excommunicationem, proprio Superiori maiori vel, si religio sit laicalis aut non exempta, Ordinario loci in quo commoratur, reservatam, ab actis legitimis ecclesiasticis est exclusus, privilegiis omnibus suae religionis privatus; et si redierit, perpetuo caret voce activa et passiva, ac praeterea aliis poenis pro gravitate culpae a Superioribus puniri debet ad normam constitutionum.[1]

When a religious gravely and contumaciously consummates[2] the crime of apostasy according to the terms of canon 644, § 1,[3] he automatically (*ipso iure*) incurs the penalties stated in canon 2385. Since by reason of their intention of not returning they commit a crime specifically distinct from flight,[4] and since a penalty as stated in the law is not incurred unless the crime is perfectly complete according to the terms of the law,[5] apostates do not also incur the penalties of fugitives.

[1] Canon 2385. Without prejudice to the prescription of canon 646, the religious who has apostatized from his institute incurs by the law itself (*ipso iure*) excommunication reserved to his own higher superior or, in the case of a lay or non-exempt institute, to the ordinary of the place in which he resides; he is excluded from all legitimate ecclesiastical acts, deprived of all the privileges of his institute; and, if he returns to it, he remains forever without active and passive voice, and, besides, he must be punished by his superiors with other penalties according to the gravity of the fault, conformably to the constitutions. (Authorized English Translation.)

[2] Canon 2242, § 1.

[3] Canon 2228. Those in temporary vows or those who as members of societies live in common without vows cannot be apostates according to the terms of canon 644, § 1.—*Supra*, pp. 54-57.

[4] *Supra*, pp. 62, 64, 73.

[5] Canon 2228.

Any cause which excuses from the imputation of the act of apostasy from a religious institute in the nature of a grave sin also excuses from the incurring of the penalties of canon 2385.[6] Passion and grave fear can do away with imputability of the crime.[7] Ignorance of the law or of the penalties, as long as it is not affected, crass or supine ignorance excuses from the excommunication but never from the vindictive penalties.[8] None of the penalties are removed by the very fact of the apostate's return. They must be absolved or dispensed by legitimate authority.[9]

"Firmo praescripto canon 646." It has been stated that the qualified crimes of apostasy from the faith, flight with a person of the other sex and the contracting or the attempt of contracting marriage offer a presumption (*hominis*) that the guilty religious has the intention of not returning to his institute.[10] The religious who commits these qualified crimes not only is automatically (*ipso facto*) dismissed,[11] not only incurs the specific penalties enacted for these crimes[12] and not only is perpetually deprived of wearing the ecclesiastical habit,[13] but also automatically (*ipso iure*) incurs the penalties of an apostate from a religious institute if he has left with the intention of not returning.

1. The Excommunication

" . . . ipso iure incurrit in excommunicationem." The chief penalty for apostasy from a religious institute is excommunication with all the effects stated in the law.[14] This excommunication is a *latae sententiae* penalty and is incurred the moment the crime is consummated,[15] *i. e.,* the moment the perpetually professed religious has

[6] Canon 2218, § 2.

[7] Canons 2205, § 2; 2206.

[8] Canon 2229, §§ 1, 3, n. 1.

[9] Smith, *The Penal Law for Religious,* p. 99.

[10] *Supra,* pp. 66, 67.

[11] Canon 646, § 1.

[12] Canons 2314, § 1, nn. 1, 2 and § 2; 2342, § 3; 2353; 2358; 2359; 2388.

[13] Canon 670.

[14] Canons 1240, § 1, n. 2; 1757, § 2, n. 1; 1758; 2259-2266; cf. Hyland, *Excommunication,* pp. 48-167.

[15] Canon 2217, § 1, n. 2.

left his religious house or place of obedience with the externally manifested intention of not returning to the institute.

"*. . . proprio Superiori maiori . . . reservatam.*" In exempt clerical institutes the excommunication for apostasy from the institute is reserved by law (*a iure*) to the proper major superior.[16]

Besides dominative power superiors in exempt clerical institutes have also jurisdiction in both forums over their subjects.[17] Therefore the major superiors and their delegates can absolve from this excommunication. Major superiors are the abbot primate, the abbot superior of a monastic congregation, the abbot of an independent (*sui iuris*) monastery even though it forms part of a monastic congregation, the superior-general of the whole institute, the provincial superior, their vicars and all others who have powers equivalent (*ad instar*) to those of provincials, *e.g.*, vice-provincials.[18]

The abbot primate and the abbot superior of a monastic congregation are major superiors, but they do not have all the powers of major superiors. They have only the powers granted to them by their constitutions and the decrees of the Holy See.[19] Whether they can absolve from the excommunication for apostasy will have to be determined by their constitutions or by the decrees of the Holy See.

Though major superiors in exempt clerical institutes are ordinaries,[20] it must be noted that, since canon 2385 states that the excommunication is reserved to the proper *major superior* not the proper *ordinary,* and since a reservation must be interpreted strictly,[21] the power of local ordinaries to absolve even peregrines from the censures which by law are reserved to the ordinary [22] is of no avail in regard to the excommunication of canon 2385, in the case of a religious of an exempt clerical institute, for the absolution from this excommunication is reserved to his own major superior.[23]

16 Canon 2385.
17 Canon 501, § 1; cf., Coronata, *Institutiones,* n. 534.
18 Canon 488, n. 8.
19 Canon 501, § 3.
20 Canon 198, § 1.
21 Canon 2246, § 2.
22 Canon 2253, n. 3.
23 Blat, *De Delictis et Poenis,* nn. 77, 228; Smith, *The Penal Law for Religious,* p. 98.

Since no distinction is made, the reservation to the proper major superiors of the institute holds even in the case when the apostate is automatically dismissed from the institute in view of the qualified crimes mentioned in canon 646, § 1.[24] The reason for this is that a dismissal does not break all the bonds with the institute [25] except in those institutes which have the privilege to the effect that dismissal includes also automatically (*ipso facto*) a dispensation from the vows. In this latter case it would seem that the excommunication of canon 2385 is not reserved to the proper major superior of the institute, but to the ordinary of the place of residence of the apostate, since the superiors of the institute no longer have jurisdiction over the former religious.

" . . . si religio sit laicalis aut non exempta, Ordinario loci in quo commoratur . . . reservatam." If the apostate belongs to a lay or to a non-exempt clerical institute, the excommunication of canon 2385 is reserved to the ordinary of the place of the apostate's stay. The reason for the reservation to the local ordinary inheres in the fact that superiors of non-exempt clerical and of lay institutes have no jurisdiction, but only dominative power, over their subjects.[26] If a lay institute is exempt, the excommunication is nevertheless reserved to the local ordinary, for canon 2385 states that in lay institutes it is reserved to the ordinary of the place and makes no distinction between exempt and non-exempt lay institutes. Moreover, if the superiors of the exempt lay institute are clerics they could be given jurisdiction; but if they are not clerics the giving of jurisdiction to them would be contrary to the present practice of the Church.[27] In either case it is not given by canon 2385 for mention is made of lay

[24] Pejska, *Jus Canonicum Religiosorum,* p. 188; Larraona, "Quaestio Canonica,"—*CpR,* IV (1923), 174-178.

[25] The prescript of canon 672, § 1, does not oblige superiors to readmit the automatically dismissed.—P. C. I., 30 iul. 1934—*AAS,* XXVI (1934), 494.

[26] Canon 501, § 1; cf., Coronata, *Institutiones,* n. 534.

[27] Saucedo, in a doctrinal dissertation presented to the Athanaeum of St. Apollinaris, contends that the lay superiors of his institute and of all exempt lay institutes enjoy jurisdiction.—"Exercitium Jurisdictionis et Superiores Laici ex Ordine Hospitalario S. Joannis de Deo,"—*CpR,* XIII (1932), 51-61, 106-114, 224-231, 291-302.

institutes without any distinction as to their exempt or non-exempt status.

In the case of nuns *(moniales)* who are subject to regulars the absolution from the excommunication for apostasy from their religious institute can be granted with equal right by the local ordinary or by the regular superior,[28] since they are subject to the jurisdiction of the regular superior by reason of their constitutions and to the local ordinary by reason of canon 2385.

The local ordinary to whom the excommunication is reserved in the case of non-exempt clerical and of lay institutes is the ordinary of the place where the religious actually is.[29] If the apostate goes from one place to another the reservation may successively pertain to various local ordinaries.[30] If he returns to a house of the institute, the reservation pertains to the ordinary of the place of that house.[31] It is not necessary that the apostate acquire a domicile or a quasi-domicile in the place.[32] Since this excommunication is reserved to the ordinary of the place where the apostate actually is, in the last analysis, it may be said to be reserved to the ordinary of the place where the apostate goes to confession.[33] However, this is not quite accurate, since absolution from the censure could be given without sacramental confession.[34]

Excommunication, being a censure or medicinal penalty,[35] is intended to break the contumacy of the delinquent.[36] Absolution from the excommunication [37] is due in justice [38] when the religious recedes from his contumacy, *i. e.*, when he repents of his crime and makes

[28] Coronata, *Institutiones*, n. 2189; Schaefer, *De Religiosis*, n. 571.

[29] Canon 2385.

[30] Schaefer, *De Religiosis*, n. 571; Cappello, *De Censuris*, n. 391; Vermeersch-Creusen, *Epitome*, I, n. 747; Coronata, *Institutiones*, I, p. 864, n. 644, nota 7; Cappello, *De Censuris*, n. 391; Blat, *De Delictis et Poenis*, n. 228.

[31] Schaefer, *loc. cit.*

[32] Cappello, *loc. cit.*

[33] Blat, *loc. cit.*

[34] Canon 2251.

[35] Canon 2255, § 1, n. 1.

[36] Canon 2241, § 1.

[37] Canon 2236, § 1.

[38] Cappello, *De Censuris*, n. 85.

satisfaction for the damage done and for the scandal, or when he has at least seriously promised to do so.[39] In the case of an apostate from a religious institute this satisfaction must include the rectifying of his status by his return to his institute, or by his serious promise to return within a fixed time, or by the obtaining of an indult of exclaustration or secularization with permission to live in the world in the interim.

Outside of the danger of death, absolution from a censure reserved by law *(a iure)* can be granted by the one who attached the censure to the law, by the one to whom it is reserved, by their superior or successor, or by one delegated by them.[40] The vicars of major superiors are also to be classed as major superiors and consequently can absolve from this excommunication in the case of exempt clerical religious. Likewise the canon penitentiary [41] and the vicar general of the local ordinary can absolve from the excommunication in the case of a lay or of a non-exempt religious, and this the vicar general can do without a special mandate.[42]

Confessors of exempt clerical religious, whether they be deputed by the superior according to canon 518, or whether they be authorized by virtue of canon 519 to hear the confession of a religious who seeks the peace of his conscience, cannot absolve from the excommunication for apostasy from a religious institute, for the power of absolving from the cases reserved in the institute which is granted to them is for cases reserved in the institute *by* the institute, and not for the cases reserved in the institute by the common law.[43]

[39] Canon 2242, § 3.

[40] Canons 2236, § 1; 2253, n. 3.

[41] Canon 401, § 1.

[42] Coronata, *Institutiones*, n. 2189; Augustine, *A Commentary*, VIII, 470.

[43] Coronata, *Institutiones*, n. 2189; Ayrinhac-Lydon, *Penal Legislation*, p. 299; Smith, *The Penal Law for Religious*, p. 98; Larraona, "Commentarium Codicis,"—*CpR*, X (1929), 445; Gomez, "Studia Canonica,"—*CpR*, VIII (1927), 364, 365; Vermeersch, "Quaeritur quinam sint casus qui, in can. 518 et 519, vocantur 'in religione' reservati?"—*Periodica*, XIX (1923), 112*-114*. Augustine (*A Commentary*, VIII [2. ed., 1924], 470) says that canon 519 cannot be used; but the same author in another place (*A Commentary*, III [4. ed., 1929], 384) states that this canon may be used by the confessor therein mentioned to grant absolution from cases reserved by the common law.

In the case of lay and of non-exempt clerical religious, inasmuch as the excommunication is reserved to the local ordinary, regular confessors and others who enjoy the privilege of absolving from censures reserved by common law to the local ordinary,[44] can grant absolution from the excommunication for apostasy from religion.

Not only in danger of death [45] but also in the more urgent cases, *i. e.*, when the censure cannot be observed without danger of grave scandal or of infamy, or when it is hard for the penitent to remain in mortal sin for the time necessary to approach the superior for the necessary faculty,[46] all confessors can absolve from the excommunication for apostasy from a religious institute according to the norm of canon 2254, § 1, both in the case of lay and of non-exempt religious when the censure is reserved to the local ordinary, and also in the case of exempt clerical religious when the censure is reserved to their proper major superior, for canon 2254 says that they can absolve from censures "no matter how they be reserved" *(quoquo modo reservatis)*.[47]

Among the dispositions which the apostate must have is the readiness to rectify his status by his return to his institute within a fixed time if he has not yet done so, or by petitioning either for an indult which will entitle him to temporary absence from the institute *(exclaustratio)* or for a dispensation from the continued observance of his religious vows *(saecularizatio)*.[48] If the superiors refuse to

[44] St. Alphonsus de Liguori, *Theologia Moralis* (ed. Gaudé, 4 vols., Romae: Typis Polyglottis Vaticanis, 1905-1912), Lib. VIII, n. 99; Coronata, *Institutiones*, n. 619b, 3; Aertyns-Damen, *Theologia Moralis*, II, n. 1067; Noldin-Schmitt, *Summa Theologiae Moralis* (3 vols., Oeniponte, Lipsiae: Rauch, Vol. I, 26. ed., 1939, Vol. II, 25. ed., 1938, Vol. III, 26. ed., 1940), I, *De Censuris*, n. 95.

[45] Canon 2252.

[46] Absolution from sin cannot be granted before absolution from excommunication. (Canons 2250, § 2; 2260, § 1.)

[47] Moriarty, *The Extraordinary Absolution from Censures*. The Catholic University of America Canon Law Studies, n. 113 (Washington, D. C.: The Catholic University of America, 1938), pp. 274, 275; Cocchi, *De Delictis et Poenis*, n. 261.

[48] Moriarty, *loc. cit.*

readmit the automatically dismissed apostate,[49] he must seek a dispensation from his vows.[50]

Since the apostate, if he has not returned to his institute, is bound to do so without delay,[51] and recourse to the ordinary or to proper major superior will ordinarily be taken care of on his return, the use of canon 2254, § 3, will be rare. If it is morally impossible for him to return to his institute, and if he is willing to have recourse and to obey the mandates of his superior or of the ordinary, canon 2254, § 1, can still be used; [52] and in the extreme case in which both return and recourse are impossible, *e. g.*, because of war or in view of his confinement in a concentration camp, canon 2254, § 3, could also be used, the confessor absolving from the excommunication and himself giving the mandates.

Regular confessors and others who by privilege can absolve from the excommunication for apostasy from a religious institute, as well as all confessors who absolve according to the norms of canon 2254, do so only in the internal sacramental forum. The religious thus absolved, if there is no scandal, can act as one who has been absolved in both forums. Superiors, however, can force the observance of the excommunication in the external forum until the religious is absolved in both forums.[53] Even before he receives absolution in the internal forum, the apostate, if no declaratory sentence has been given, is excused from observing the excommunication if he cannot do so without infamy.[54] Before the declaratory sentence has been given no one can force him to observe the excommunication in the external forum unless his crime is notorious.[55]

On the occasion of jubilee years it has been the practice of the popes to grant faculties for the absolution of the excommunication of apostates from religious institutes.[56] This practice was followed

[49] P. C. I., 30 iul. 1934—*AAS*, XXVI (1934), 494.

[50] Moriarty, *op. cit.*, p. 276.

[51] Canon 645, § 1.

[52] Moriarty, *op. cit.*, pp. 275, 276.

[53] Canon 2251.

[54] Canon 2232, § 1.

[55] Canons 2197, nn. 2, 3; 2232, § 1.

[56] *Supra*, pp. 45, 46, 49, 50.

by Pius XI on the occasion of the jubilee years of 1925, 1926, 1929, 1933 and 1934. However, on the occasion of each of these jubilees confessors had to examine both the faculties as given to them in the apostolic constitutions concerning the jubilee and also the *monita* of the Sacred Penitentiary concerning the use of these faculties. The confessor had to act according to his delegation. He had to observe the solemnities and had to prescribe the various conditions which were enjoined by the Holy See.[57] The following explanation of the use of jubilee faculties is based on the faculties given on the occasion of the jubilee years proclaimed by Pius XI.

On the occasion of the jubilee years of 1925 and 1933 the pope gave the minor penitentiaries and other confessors *in Urbe* the faculty to absolve, in the jubilee confession and in the internal sacramental forum only, from censures reserved by law to the ordinary; [58] and in the extension of the jubilees to the whole world the pope gave the same faculty to all confessors.[59] Since these constitutions gave the faculty only for censures reserved by law to the *ordinary,* apostate religious of exempt clerical institutes could not have been absolved by reason of these faculties, for their excommunication was reserved to their "proper major superior" and reservations are subject to a strict interpretation.[60] It might be argued that their major superiors are ordinaries [61] and that, since the jubilee faculties are privileges [62] and receive a wide interpretation,[63] these faculties should include the power to absolve from censures reserved explicitly to major superiors for they are ordinaries in exempt clerical institutes.[64]

[57] Maroto, "Brevis Expositio Constitutionis Apostolicae 'Auspicantibus Nobis,' "—*Apollinaris,* II (1929), 197, 198.

[58] Pius XI, const. *Si umquam,* 15 iul. 1924, §§ VI, XVI, n. 1—*AAS,* XVI (1924), 309-316; const. *Indicto a Nobis,* 30 ian. 1933—*AAS,* XXV (1933), 14-19.

[59] Pius XI, const. *Servatoris Iesu Christi,* 25 dec. 1925, § 3—*AAS,* XVII (1925), 611-618; const. *Quod superiore,* 2 apr. 1934, § VIII, n. 3—*AAS,* XXVI (1934), 137-148.

[60] Canon 2246, § 2.

[61] Canon 198, § 1.

[62] Canon 66, § 1.

[63] Canons 50; 68.

[64] Canon 198, § 1.

On the occasion of the extraordinary jubilee of 1929 the pope gave all confessors the faculty to absolve in both internal forums for all cases reserved by law (except censures *specialissimo modo* reserved to the Holy See and the censure for the violation of the secrecy of the Holy Office), and he made no specific mention of the persons or authorities to whom the censures were reserved.[65] Since no mention was made of the one to whom the censure was reserved, confessors could have absolved even exempt clerical religious from the excommunication for apostasy from their religious institute.

The *monita* of the Sacred Penitentiary issued in 1924 and in 1934 stated that apostates from religious institutes could not be absolved while they remained outside of their institute, unless they had the firm proposal of returning within a fixed time. If this proposal was left unexecuted through their fault they fell back into the same kind of censure from which they were previously absolved. The *monita* also stated that such religious apostates were to be warned that as long as they remained outside of their religious house they were excluded from all the legitimate ecclesiastical acts, deprived of the privileges of their institute, and subject to the local ordinary.[66] The *monitum* of 1924 added that an apostate who had committed the qualified crimes mentioned in canon 646 could be absolved in the internal forum, but the whole matter was to be sent to the Sacred Penitentiary, which would refer it to the Holy Office for opportune remedies. In § X the Sacred Penitentiary stated that, if the apostate indicated his desire of seeking from his superior before his return to the institute a mitigation of the penalties to be imposed, he could not be absolved by the confessor.

Finally, if the apostate remains under the excommunication for one year he becomes suspect of heresy; [67] the local ordinary, even in the case of exempt religious,[68] and the Holy Office can proceed

[65] Pius XI, const. *Auspicantibus Nobis*, 6 ian. 1929—*AAS*, XXI (1929), 5-11.

[66] S. Poenit., 31 iul. 1924, § IX—*AAS*, XVI (1924), 337-344; 3 apr. 1934, § IX—*AAS*, XXVI (1934), 149-152.

[67] Canon 2340, § 1.

[68] Canon 616, § 2.

against him according to the norm of canon 2315,[69] but not the superiors of the religious since they may not interfere in matters pertaining to the Holy Office.[70]

2. The Exclusion from the Exercise of the Legitimate Ecclesiastical Acts

"*. . . ipso iure . . . ab actis legitimis ecclesiasticis est exclusus.*" By the very act of apostasy *(ipso iure)*, *i. e.*, the moment the religious consummates the crime, he is excluded from the exercise of the legitimate ecclesiastical acts. By legitimate acts are meant: the administration of ecclesiastical goods; the acting in ecclesiastical processes as judge, auditor, relator, defender of the bond, promotor of justice or of the faith, courier, chancellor, notary, beadle, advocate or proxy; the acting as godparent in baptism or in confirmation; the casting of a vote in an ecclesiastical election; and the right of patronage.[71]

Since the penalty of the exclusion from the exercise of the legitimate ecclesiastical acts in specifically mentioned in canon 2385 it must be concluded that it is not the effect of the excommunication that is indicated but the vindictive penalty [72] and since no time is fixed for its dispensation, the penalty endures until it is dispensed by competent authority.[73] It cannot be argued that, since the mention of this penalty as well as of the penalty of privation of privileges is placed in canon 2385 before the words "*et si redierit,*" these penalties do not bind after the apostate returns. If this were true, then the explicit mention of exclusion from the exercise of the legitimate acts and the indication of the privation of privileges would not be necessary, for the apostate in view of his excommunication is already excluded from the exercise of the legitimate acts and is prohibited

[69] The local ordinary or the Holy Office will warn the excommunicated apostate and, if he does not amend within six months after the warning, he is subject to the penalties for heresy.

[70] Canon 501, § 2.

[71] Canon 2256, n. 2.

[72] Canon 2291, n. 8.

[73] Smith, *The Penal Law for Religious*, p. 99.

from enjoying his privileges,[74] and in the ordinary case is not absolved from the excommunication until he returns. Therefore it must be concluded that the penalty of exclusion from the exercise of the legitimate acts binds even after the apostate returns until he is dispensed by competent authority.[75]

In practice this means that, though they can be appointed as superiors or as economes or as other officials charged with the administration of the goods of the institute, yet they could not licitly exercise this administration even as a member of a board or council [76] until they are dispensed; and if those who hold such offices become apostates, on their return they are likewise excluded from the licit administration of the goods of the institute until they are dispensed. The same may be said of the licit exercise of the other legitimate acts from which they are excluded.

Some legitimate acts include a participation in ecclesiastical jurisdiction and are offices in the strict sense; all are offices in the wide sense, since they are functions exercised for a spiritual end.[77] The offices are not lost by exclusion from the exercise of the legitimate acts, but their use is rendered gravely illicit. Acts placed by those who are excluded from the exercise of the legitimate acts are valid, but they are illicit unless there is a just cause to warrant their exercise.[78] The religious can, after an unheeded warning, be deprived of the office in view of his grave violation of the common life by the act of apostasy.[79]

Since the exclusion from the exercise of the legitimate acts is not a penalty of privation nor of incapacitation for offices, the power of ordinaries, local and proper, to dispense from the penalty is not restricted by canon 2237, § 1, n. 3. Hence ordinaries, local and proper, can dispense from this penalty in both public and occult cases.[80]

[74] Canon 2263.

[75] Smith, *loc. cit.*

[76] Blat, *De Delictis et Poenis*, n. 81; Hyland, *Excommunication*, p. 128.

[77] Canon 145, § 1; cf. Hyland, *op. cit.*, pp. 127, 128.

[78] Cappello, *De Censuris*, n. 150; Coronata, *Institutiones*, n. 1776; Hyland, *op. cit.*, p. 128.

[79] Canon 2389.

[80] Canon 2237.

If the penalty cannot be observed without infamy and the crime is not notorious, then the religious is excused from observing the penalty as long as a declaratory sentence has not been rendered.[81] In the more urgent occult cases confessors can suspend the penalty if it cannot be observed without scandal or infamy. They must, however, impose the obligation of having recourse within a month to the Sacred Penitentiary or the ordinary and of observing his mandates. In the extraordinary case wherein recourse is impossible the confessor can dispense and can himself give the mandates according to the norm of canon 2254, § 3.[82]

3. The Privation of All the Privileges of the Institute

". . . ipso iure . . . privilegiis omnibus suae religionis privatus." By the excommunication which the apostate incurs he is prohibited from using *all* privileges.[83] The privileges are not lost, but their use is rendered illicit.[84] By this additional penalty as it is stated in canon 2385 the apostate *loses* all the spiritual (*e. g.*, indulgences) and temporal privileges of his institute, both those which are common to all religious and those which are particular to his institute,[85] even the privilege of exemption if he belongs to an order or to an exempt congregation.[86]

Schaefer [87] and Fanfani [88] state that the apostate is also deprived of the suffrages of the institute. The Code always distinguishes between privileges and suffrages [89] and, as Fanfani says elsewhere,

[81] Canon 2232, § 1.

[82] Canon 2290.

[83] Canon 2263.

[84] Vermeersch-Creusen, *Epitome*, III, n. 465.

[85] Schaefer, *De Religiosis*, n. 571.

[86] Blat, *De Delictis et Poenis*, n. 228. Exempt religious illegitimately outside their religious house do not enjoy the privilege of exemption (Canon 616, § 1). Thus fugitives do not enjoy exemption, but are deprived of it as are apostates.

[87] *De Religiosis*, p. 980, n. 571, note 165.

[88] *De Iure Religiosorum*, n. 494.

[89] Canons 567, § 1; 578, n. 1; 2262, § 1; 2263.

suffrages are not privileges but a kind of acquired right.[90] Since canon 2385 is a penal law, it must be interpreted strictly,[91] and the deprivation of privileges does not therefore include a loss of the suffrages.

Augustine says that apostates from religious institutes are not deprived of the privileges of the clerical state.[92] It would be more proper to say that all religious lose the clerical privileges which they enjoy as religious,[93] but religious who are moreover clerics still enjoy them by reason of their clerical state.

As has been stated in regard to the vindictive penalty of exclusion from the legitimate acts,[94] so in regard to the deprivation of privileges the penalty is not taken away by the very fact of the apostate's return.[95] The question arises as to who can dispense from this penalty after the apostate has returned. The privileges of a religious institute are granted by the Holy See. Ordinaries do not have this power of dispensing in public cases (and this is usual with apostasy) when there is question of the penalty of privation of a privilege granted by the Holy See.[96] But it seems that, since the privileges of which the apostate is deprived by canon 2385 were granted not to the individual religious but to the institute and inasmuch as the religious enjoys them only mediately, the ordinary (local ordinaries in the case of non-exempt religious, major superiors in the case of exempt clerical religious), can dispense from this penalty of deprivation of privileges. This seems to be the reason why Smith says that all the vindictive penalties except the perpetual loss of electoral rights can be dispensed by the ordinary.[97] In the more urgent occult cases any confessor can dispense according to the norm of canon 2290.

[90] *Op. cit.*, n. 482.

[91] Canon 19.

[92] *A Commentary,* VIII, 470.

[93] Canon 614.

[94] *Supra,* p. 89.

[95] Smith, *The Penal Law for Religious,* p. 99.

[96] Canon 2237, § 1, n. 3.

[97] *Loc. cit.*

4. The Perpetual Loss of Electoral Rights

"*. . . et si redierit, perpetuo caret voce activa et passiva.*" By reason of the excommunication [98] and by reason of the exclusion from the licit exercise of the legitimate ecclesiastical acts consequent on the excommunication [99] the apostate from a religious institute may not licitly, and after a declaratory sentence has been rendered validly, cast a vote.[100] Moreover, because of his excommunication he may not licitly obtain either by election or appointment any office or function in the Church. After a declaratory sentence has been rendered he cannot validly obtain them.[101] Hence an apostate from his religious institute cannot licitly (or validly if a declaratory sentence has been rendered) elect or be elected or be appointed to any office or function *(munus)* in his institute. By the absolution from the excommunication all these penalties would cease without further dispensation [102] if it were not for the further provisions of canon 2385.

The apostate from his religious institute is excluded from the licit exercise of the legitimate ecclesiastical acts by canon 2385. Among these acts is the right to cast a vote. Since this penalty is a vindictive penalty it is not dispensed by the fact of the absolution from the excommunication, nor by the very fact of the apostate's return.[103]

Moreover, the religious by the very act of apostasy from his religious institute incurs not only the exclusion from the licit exercise of the right to vote, but is perpetually *deprived* of all active and passive electoral rights.[104] After the apostate returns to the institute he cannot validly vote in the chapters of the institute, nor can he validly be elected to an office [105] that is obtained through an election.

[98] Canon 2265, § 1, n. 1.

[99] Canon 2263.

[100] Canon 2265, § 2.

[101] Canon 2265, § 1, n. 2 and § 2.

[102] Coronata, *Institutiones,* n. 1776.

[103] *Supra,* pp. 79, 89, 91.

[104] Canon 2385. The active electoral right denotes the right to vote, the passive electoral right signifies the capacity of being a candidate for election.

[105] Office here is taken in the wide sense of any function (*munus*) in the institute (canon 145), since this penalty is inflicted not only on exempt clerical religious but also on non-exempt clerical and on lay religious who do not enjoy jurisdiction over their subjects.

After the excommunication of the apostate is absolved he can be given an office or a function that is conferred by appointment; [106] and in the case of offices or functions conferred by election he can be postulated [107] according to the norms of law.[108] If the postulation is admitted by the Holy See, then it seems that also the active electoral right is restored.[109]

In the event that one who is deprived of the active electoral right is admitted to an election his vote is invalid, but the election itself is valid unless it is evident that the person elected would not have otherwise received the requisite number of votes.[110]

It must be noted that an apostate woman religious after her return retains the right to vote for the reappointment of an ordinary confessor for a second and third triennium, for in this matter even those who do not enjoy the right of voting in other affairs are granted that right by the law.[111]

Whenever the crime of apostasy from a religious institute is a public crime according to the norm of canon 2197, n. 1, ordinaries, local or proper as the case may be, cannot dispense from the penalty of the perpetual privation of electoral rights.[112] Such a dispensation can be granted only by the Holy See.[113] However, if an occult case of apostasy should arise, the ordinaries have the power to dispense from this penalty,[114] and in the more urgent occult cases any confessor has a like power according to the norm of canon 2290.

5. The Punishments After Return to the Institute

"*. . . et si redierit . . . practerea aliis poenis pro gravitate culpae a Superioribus puniri debet ad normam constitutionum.* The superiors who in law are authorized to inflict the punishments on the

[106] Schaefer, *De Religiosis,* n. 571.
[107] Coronata, *Institutiones,* n. 2189; Schaefer, *op. cit.,* n. 571.
[108] Canons 179-182.
[109] Coronata, *loc. cit.*; Augustine, *A Commentary,* VIII, 470, 471.
[110] Canon 167, § 2.
[111] Canon 526.
[112] Canon 2237, § 1, n. 3.
[113] Smith, *The Penal Law for Religious,* p. 99.
[114] Canon 2237, § 2.

apostate who returns to his institute are the major and local superiors, according to the constitutions of the institute, since the Code makes no reservation in favor of the major superiors. Local ordinaries are not the superiors of religious [115] and are not permitted to inflict these punishments on the returned apostates.

Since the inflicting of punishments is committed to the superiors of all institutes, and the superiors of lay and of non-exempt clerical institutes do not enjoy strictly so called jurisdiction over their subjects,[116] it seems that the word "penalties" *(poenis)* is not to be taken in the strict sense of canonical penalties, but may be taken to denote any punitive measures inflicted by a superior in virtue of his dominative power.[117] Superiors of exempt clerical institutes can inflict strict canonical penalties, penances and penal remedies.[118] If strict canonical penalties are inflicted, they are *ferendae sententiae* penalties and are imposed *ab homine,* and hence they are reserved to the superior who inflicts them or to his superior, successor or delegate.[119]

The obligation of the superiors to inflict punishments on returned apostates is a mandatory one. This is evident from the words "must be punished" *(puniri debet)*.[120] Though these punishments may not under all circumstances be strict canonical penalties, yet it seems that the same norms can be applied, namely, it is committed to the prudence of the superior to postpone their infliction, or to abstain entirely from inflicting them, or to temper them according to the norm of canon 2223, § 2.

The punishments are to be inflicted according to the norm of the constitutions. Many of the constitutions merely restate the prescriptions of the Code in regard to apostates and fugitives; others specifically state the punishments that are to be inflicted after the apostate returns. Thus the constitutions of the Friars Minor state that "the principal punishments for apostates and fugitives are: detention in a convent without permission to go out; a spiritual retreat; the last

115 Except the abbot of a territorially independent abbey (*abbatia nullius*).

116 Canon 501, § 1.

117 Coronata, *Institutiones,* n. 534; Fanfani, *De Iure Religiosorum,* n. 55.

118 Canons 2306, 2313.

119 Canons 2217, § 1, n. 3; 2236, § 1.

120 Smith, *The Penal Law for Religious,* p. 99.

place among equals; suspension; and other graver punishments, regard being had for the gravity of the sin, the length of time and the crimes committed outside the cloister." [121] The constitutions of the Friars Minor Conventual state that the other punishments for apostates besides those stated in the law are: suspension *a divinis* for a time proportionate to the length of time he was contumacious; fast on bread and water for six days; and from that time he shall take the last place among those of the same rank, *i. e.*, a priest the last place among the priests, a cleric the last among the clerics, and a lay brother the last place among the lay brothers. If the religious lives a praiseworthy life for ten years after his return he can be restored by the superior-general to all things except the active and passive electoral rights in the order. The superior-general can augment or lessen the penalties according to the lesser or greater penitence of the religious. Superiors who are negligent in inflicting these penalties can be punished and can even be deprived of their office.[122] The constitutions of the Calced Carmelites state that the returned apostate and fugitive are to be deprived of their place at least for as long a time as they were out of the religious house.[123] The constitutions of the Dominicans state that during the time of penance the returned apostate shall take the last place among equals and shall fast on bread and water two days each week for a year. After the time of penance he shall not return to his former place unless he has been dispensed by the Master of the order, or by the definitors of the general or provincial chapter; but this dispensation shall not be given before the lapse of at least three years, and then the time during which he was an apostate is not counted in reckoning his place.[124]

Larraona says that, though the privation of precedence is not automatically and by the rigor of the law applied to apostates and fugitives, it can and usually is applied *ab homine*. He adds that the

[121] *The Rule and General Constitutions of the Friars Minor*, n. 383.

[122] *Constitutiones Ordinis Fratrum Minorum Sancti Francisci Conventualium* (Romae, 1932), n. 817-819.

[123] *Constitutiones Ordinis Fratrum B. V. M. de Monte Carmelo* (Vatican City, 1930), Art. 297.

[124] *Constitutiones Fratrum S. Ordinis Praedicatorum*, const. 961.

privation of precedence in the internal penal law of religious is a most grave penalty, especially if it is perpetual, and is not generally applied except for the graver crimes.[125]

If no punishments are stated in the constitutions the superiors can impose punishments by reason of the dominative power which they have over their subjects. Superiors of exempt religious can, moreover, inflict strict canonical penances and penal remedies, or even penalties acording to the norm of canon 2222, § 1, if there is scandal or special gravity attached to the transgression.

In the application of punishments superiors are to proceed according to the gravity of the crime *(pro gravitate culpae)*, taking into consideration the circumstances of the apostate's leaving, his conduct while absent, the amount of time that he was away and the repentance with which he returned. They should be mindful of the admonition of the Council of Trent quoted in canon 2214, § 2, that, "when the rod must be used, rigor should be tempered with meekness, judgment with mercy, and severity with mildness."

6. Cooperators

The question arises as to cooperators in the crime of apostasy from a religious institute. Canon 2231 states that when several concur in the commission of a crime after the manner delineated in canon 2209, §§ 1-3, *i. e.*, as cooperators without whose cooperation the crime would not have been committed, they incur the same penalty unless the contrary be expressly stated in the law. Therefore it must be concluded that such cooperators in the crime of apostasy incur the same penalties as the apostates themselves, at least those penalties which can be incurred by them.[126] Thus other religious, even though they be not members of the same institute to which the apostate belongs, incur all the penalties stated in canon 2385. Clerics who are not religious and also laymen incur the excommunication, the exclusion from the licit exercise of the legitimate ecclesiastical acts and the privation of active and passive electoral rights. Ignorance of the law or of the penalties, although it is not to be pre-

[125] "Commentarium Codicis"—*CpR*, IV (1923), 331-335, n. I.
[126] Schaefer, *De Religiosis*, n. 572.

sumed,[127] as long as it is not affected, crass or supine ignorance, excuses from the excommunication but never from the vindictive penalties.[128]

In the case of apostasy accompanied by flight with a person of the other sex, if both parties are apostate religious they both incur the penalties twice, once by reason of apostasy from their own institute, and once by their effective cooperation in the apostasy of the other party, for ordinarily there are as many penalties as there are crimes committed.[129]

7. The Declaratory Sentence

Lastly there is the obligation of the ordinary, local or proper as the case may be,[130] to render a declaratory sentence in the case.[131] Canon 2232, § 1, states that *latae sententiae* penalties immediately bind the delinquent in both forums, but before the declaratory sentence is rendered the delinquent is excused from observing them if he cannot do so without infamy, and no one can force him to do so in the external forum unless his crime is notorious. In most cases apostasy from religion is notorious by notoriety of fact, *i. e.,* the crime is public and occurs in such circumstances that it cannot be concealed by any artifice or excused by any legal assumption.[132]

However, canon 2232, § 1, employs the phrase "without prejudice to canon 2223, § 4," which canon states that it is left to the prudence of the superior to declare a *latae sententiae* penalty, but that when the common good demands it the sentence *must* be rendered. In the cases of apostasy from religion the common good seems to demand the declaratory sentence. First, if the excommunicated apostate illicitly exercises the power of orders or the power of jurisdiction while

[127] Canon 16, § 2.

[128] Canon 2229, §§ 1, 3, n. 1.

[129] Canon 2224, § 1.

[130] If an exempt religious commits a crime, and apostasy is a continuous crime if the apostate disregards the warnings of his superiors (Oesterle, "Casus in Canonem 2385,"—*Apollinaris,* X [1937], 124-132), local ordinaries can punish him (canon 616, § 2).

[131] A declaratory sentence is not to be confused with the declaration of fact which must be given in the case of automatic dismissal (Canon 646, § 2).

[132] Canon 2197, n. 3.

he is outside of his religious house he should be prevented from doing so. Roberti says that superiors must demand that notorious excommunicated clerics abstain from exercising jurisdiction.[133] Secondly, since legitimate ecclesiastical acts are public acts, those who are excluded from performing them should be prevented from doing so. Thirdly, active and passive electoral rights are surely things which concern the common good of the institute,[134] since the ballot which is cast by the religious in question here is invalid,[135] and since the election is invalid if his ballot is decisive for the outcome of the election [136] or if he himself be elected.[137] Moreover, if the electoral college knowingly *(scienter)* elects him it loses for that instance the right of election.[138]

From the crime arises the option of a penal action to declare the penalties.[139] If the apostate has not returned, his crime is continuous and the possibility of opening penal action is not ruled out by the factor of legal prescription; but if he has returned to his religious institute and the ordinaries do not render the declaratory sentence for the vindictive penalties, then the option of penal action is ruled out after three years by way of legal prescription.[140]

It must be admitted that, in the case of an apostate who has not yet returned, but who also is not violating the prohibitions which are binding upon him, any advantage in rendering the declaratory sentence appears rather slight. But in the case of one who has returned to the institute the desired advantage is greater. If his crime was notorious, then the superiors can force him to observe the penal-

133 *De Delictis et Poenis,* Vol. II, pars I (Romae: Apud Aedes Facultatis Iuridicae ad S. Apollinaris, 1930), n. 328.

134 Oesterle, "Casus in Canonem 2385,"—*Apollinaris,* X (1937), 124-132.

135 Canon 167, § 2.

136 Canon 167, § 2.

137 Parsons, *Canonical Elections,* The Catholic University of America Canon Law Studies, n. 118 (Washington, D. C.: The Catholic University of America, 1939), pp. 197, 198.

138 Canon 2391, § 1. One who is impeded from being elected may be postulated (canon 179, § 1), and if the votes are cast according to the formula "I elect or postulate," the election or postulation is valid (canon 180, § 2).

139 Canon 2210, § 1, n. 1.

140 Canon 1703.

ties.[141] But if his crime was occult, or if it was public but not notorious, what is there that will effectively prevent him from exercising the legitimate ecclesiastical acts, from using the privileges of his institute, and especially from voting in an election in which surely his ballot if not also the election will be invalid? Therefore it seems that if the crime was public the ordinary should proceed to render the declaratory sentence to provide for the common good. But what is to be done if his crime was occult,[142] since occult crimes are not the object of a judicial sentence? That the crime of apostasy from a religious institute is in reality occult constitutes a rare but nevertheless possible occurrence. Such a case would occur if a missionary who is often away from the house, on some definite occasion left with the intention of not returning, but after a few days repented and returned, and few if any but the superior knew of his crime. If two witnesses knew of the crime the ordinary could begin an inquisitory process, for public crimes in the sense of canon 2197, n. 1, are necessary for the beginning of such a process.[143] By thus bringing the case to the ecclesiastical forum the crime becomes public,[144] and since two sworn reliable witnesses are sufficient for establishing proof in a trial [145] the ordinary can then begin the criminal process. If the ordinary does not wish to do this he can allow the crime to remain occult and declare the penalties after the manner of a precept according to the norm of canon 2225, *i. e.*, it shall be done either in writing of before two witnesses. In practice the method that would best save the good name of the religious appears to consist in the fact that the ordinary will absolve the repentant religious from the excommunication and dispense him from all the other penalties according to canon 2237, § 2; and in the more urgent cases all confessors could absolve from the excommunication according to canon 2254 and dispense from the other penalties according to canon 2290.

[141] Canon 2232, § 1.

[142] An occult crime is one that is not public, *i. e.*, one that is not yet divulged and that in all likelihood will not become divulged. It is materially occult if the act of the crime itself is not known, formally occult if the imputability of the act in its nature of a crime is not known—(canon 2197).

[143] Coronata, *Institutiones*, n. 1452.

[144] Blat, *De Delictis et Poenis*, n. 9.

[145] Canon 1791, § 2.

CHAPTER X

THE PENALTIES INCURRED BY FUGITIVES FROM RELIGIOUS INSTITUTES

Canon 2386. Religiosus fugitivus ipso facto incurrit in privationem officii, si quod in religione habeat, et in suspensionem proprio Superiori maiori reservatam, si sit in sacris; cum autem redierit, puniatur secundum constitutiones, et si constitutiones nihil de hoc caveant, Superior maior pro gravitate culpae poenas infligat.[1]

As soon as the religious or member of a clerical society whose members live in common without vows certainly and externally consummates [2] the crime of flight, *i. e.*, as soon as he unlawfully leaves his religious house, or the place assigned to him through obedience, with the intention of deserting the institute or society for a time and of later returning to it, he *ipso facto* incurs the penalties enacted in canon 2386. He must intend to be absent for a time sufficient to constitute him a fugitive. This amount of time must be determined by the constitutions. If they make no such provision it must be determined according to the common opinion of the authors, who quite generally point to a period of about three days.[3] Any cause which excuses from the imputation of the absence in the nature of a grave sin [4] also excuses from the penalties enacted for flight from a religious institute in canon 2386.[5] Even if the act of absence remains

[1] Canon 2386. The fugitive religious incurs *ipso facto* privation of office, if he had one in his institute, and if he is in sacred orders, suspension reserved to his own higher superior; when he will have returned, he must be punished conformably to the constitutions, and if the constitutions make no provision for the case, the higher superior shall inflict punishment according to the gravity of the fault. (Authorized English Translation.)

[2] Cf. canons 2228; 2242, § 1.

[3] *Supra*, p. 75.

[4] Canons 2201-2206.

[5] Cf. canon 2218, § 2.

gravely sinful, passion, grave fear and ignorance, as long as the latter is not affected, crass or supine, can and generally do excuse from the suspension, but not from the contraction of the vindictive penalty of privation of office, nor from the punishments for which the fugitive is liable upon his return. It may also be noted that not even Cerato [6] or Cipollini [7] excuse women religious from the penalties of canon 2386.

As has been stated, members of societies who live in common without vows can be fugitives.[8] Certainly members, both clerical and lay, of *clerical* societies who live in common without vows are bound by the penalties of canon 2386.[9] But it is doubtful if members of lay societies who live in common without vows are subject to the penalties of this canon, since the interpretation of the Pontifical Commission refers only to clerical societies. The authors dispute whether the interpretation of the Pontifical Commission is extensive [10] or merely declaratory, inasmuch as whoever is bound by a prescriptive or a prohibitive law is bound also to its penal sanction.[11]

If the interpretation of the Pontifical Commission is extensive, then the members of lay societies who live in common without vows are not bound by the penalties of canon 2386. But if the interpretation is merely declaratory, *i. e.*, if it but points out what is already clearly stated in the law, then it follows that members of lay societies also are bound by the penalties, for they are bound by the prescriptive law.[12] Though the more probable opinion seems to be that the interpretation of the Pontifical Commission is merely declaratory,

[6] *Censurae Vigentes*, p. 221.

[7] *De Censuris*, n. 116.

[8] *Supra*, p. 71.

[9] P. C. I., 2-3 iun. 1918, ad VI—*AAS*, X (1918), 347.

[10] Thus: Coronata, *Institutiones*, I, p. 863, n. 642, nota 3; Chelodi-Dalpiaz, *Ius Poenale*, p. 141, n. 101, nota 1; Cappello, *De Censuris*, n. 539; Blat, *Ius de Religiosis*, n. 654; Cocchi, *De Delictis et Poenis*, n. 262; Berutti, *De Religiosis*, n. 189.

[11] Schaefer, *De Religiosis*, n. 610; Goyeneche, *De Religiosis*, p. 202, n. 102, nota 44; Maroto, "Annotationes,"—*CpR*, I (1920), 97-107.

[12] *Supra*, p. 71. The reason given by the Pontifical Commission for applying the penalties of canon 2386 to members of clerical societies, *i. e.*, "in as far as they lead a common life," is applicable also to lay societies.

yet, because of the extrinsic authority of those who hold that the interpretation is extensive, it cannot be held with certainty that members of lay societies who live in common without vows are bound by the penalties of canon 2386, for in regard to penalties it is always the more benign interpretation that is to be used.[13]

1. The Privation of Office

"*. . . ipso facto incurrit in privationem officii si quod in religione habeat.*" The penalty of privation of office is a vindictive penalty,[14] and is automatically *(ipso facto)* incurred the moment the religious or member of a clerical society who lives in common without vows has consummated the crime of flight from his religious institute or society provided that he held an office in his institute or society.

Since from the context of this canon it is evident [15] that even lay religious who have no jurisdiction are subject to the penalties, the term "office" is not to be taken in the strict sense of an ecclesiastical office to which is attached some power of orders or of jurisdiction,[16] but in the wide sense of any function legitimately exercised for a spiritual end.[17] The term therefore connotes not only the offices of major and local superiors, no matter by what title they may be designated, but also the offices held by such agents as procurators, economes, consultors, porters, assistants, parochial vicars at religious parochial benefices, etc.[18]

The dispensation from this penalty in public cases is reserved to the Holy See,[19] and in occult cases to the ordinary.[20] In the more urgent occult cases all confessors can dispense according to the norms of canon 2290. Though the religious is deprived of all the offices

[13] Canon 2219, § 1.

[14] Canon 2291, n. 10; cf. Smith, *The Penal Law for Religious,* p. 101.

[15] Canon 145, § 2.

[16] Canon 145, § 1.

[17] Coronata, *Institutiones,* n. 2191; Cocchi, *De Delictis et Poenis,* n. 262; Augustine, *A Commentary,* VIII, 472.

[18] Coronata, *loc. cit.*; Augustine, *loc. cit.*

[19] Canon 2237, § 1.

[20] Canon 2237, § 2.

which he may have been holding in the institute prior to his departure, he is not rendered incapable of being elected or appointed to the same or to different offices after his return and after his absolution from the suspension if he has incurred it.

2. The Suspension

"*. . . ipso facto incurrit . . . in suspensionem proprio Superiori maiori reservatam, si sit in sacris.*" By the very fact *(ipso facto)* of committing the crime of flight the fugitive who has sacred orders automatically incurs suspension. This suspension is a censure [21] and is incurred only by those who are in sacred orders, *i. e.*, by subdeacons, deacons and priests. It is not incurred by lay religious nor by clerics in minor orders. This suspension is a general suspension. It forbids the exercise of all acts of orders and of jurisdiction,[22] and the fugitive is subject to the comprehensive effects of suspension as they are enumerated in canons 2279-2284.

In exempt clerical institutes the absolution of this suspension is reserved to the proper major superiors of the fugitive.[23] Since the Code states that the absolution from the suspension is reserved to the proper major superior, and makes no distinction between exempt clerical religious on the one hand, and lay and non-exempt religious on the other, as it does in canon 2385, the following question arises: To whom is the censure reserved in the case of lay and of non-exempt clerical institutes and in the case of clerical societies whose members live in common without vows, for the superiors of these institutes and societies do not ordinarily have jurisdiction but only dominative power over their subjects.[24] Since the Code, with set

[21] Schaefer, *De Religiosis*, n. 572; Cappello, *De Censuris*, n. 539; Coronata, *Institutiones*, n. 2191; Vermeersch-Creusen, *Epitome*, III, n. 590; Cerato, *Censurae Vigentes*, p. 221; Cipollini, *De Censuris*, p. 221; Smith, *The Penal Law for Religious*, p. 101; Moriarty, *The Extraordinary Absolution from Censures*, p. 277; Rainer, *Suspension of Clerics*, The Catholic University of America Canon Law Studies, n. 111 (Washington, D. C.: The Catholic University of America, 1937), p. 235.

[22] Canon 2278, § 2.

[23] Canon 488, n. 8.

[24] Canon 501, § 1.

purpose,[25] makes no distinction, and since the superiors of non-exempt *clerical* institutes and societies are capable of enjoying jurisdiction, if they are clerics,[26] the authors say that in such institutes and societies the absolution from this suspension is reserved to the major superiors, who can absolve from it in view of the delegation by law *(a iure)* which they receive through canon 2386.[27] Beste says that both this opinion and also the one which holds that the absolution is reserved to the local ordinary in all the cases except those in which the fugitives belong to exempt clerical institutes are probable.[28] Woywod, however, says that the opinion which reserves this censure to the local ordinary for its absolution is preferable.[29] Others say absolutely that in all cases except those which affect exempt clerical religious the censure is reserved to the local ordinary.[30]

In regard to lay institutes[31] distinctions are necessary. If the major superior of a lay institute is a cleric, and therefore is capable of enjoying jurisdiction,[32] there is no reason to deny him the same delegation by law *(a iure)* that is conceded to major superiors of clerical institutes and societies by canon 2386.[33] If the major superior of a lay institute is a laic, another distinction is necessary. If the institute is non-exempt, then the suspension incurred by cleri-

[25] Vermeersch-Creusen, *Epitome*, III, n. 590.

[26] Canon 118.

[27] Schaefer, *De Religiosis*, n. 572; Goyeneche, *De Religiosis*, p. 204, nota 52; Coronata, *Institutiones*, I, p. 865, n. 644, nota 7; IV, p. 631, n. 2191; Blat, *De Delictis et Poenis*, n. 229; Beste, *Introductio in Codicem*, p. 969; Ayrinhac-Lydon, *Penal Legislation*, p. 300; Vermeersch-Creusen, *loc. cit.*

[28] *Loc. cit.*

[29] "Apostasy from Religious Life,"—*HPR*, XXXIX (1938-1939), 264-274.

[30] Chelodi-Dalpiaz, *Ius Poenale*, p. 141, n. 101, nota 2; Ayrinhac-Lydon, *Penal Legislation*, p. 300; Fanfani, *De Iure Religiosorum*, n. 494.

[31] A religious institute is clerical if many of the members have received o. should, according to the constitutions, receive the priesthood; otherwise it is lay (canon 488, n. 4). In both clerical and lay institutes there can be both clerical and lay members. The character of the institute is not determined by the alternate fact of being ruled by a clerical or a lay superior, but by the status which actually does or should attach to the majority of the members.—Schaefer, *De Religiosis*, n. 51, 4.

[32] Canon 118.

[33] Goyeneche, *De Religiosis*, p. 204, n. 102, nota 52.

cal members who become fugitives is reserved for its absolution to the local ordinary, since the major superiors as laics are incapable of jurisdiction according to the common law.[34] However, it is not impossible that major superiors of even such institutes may be granted jurisdiction by canon 2386 contrary to the usual practice of the common law. Coronata says that even in non-exempt institutes the suspension is reserved to the major superior,[35] and he makes no distinction so as to exclude the major superiors of a lay institute.

Lastly, there is the question of exempt lay institutes whose major superiors are laics. As has been stated Saucedo, in a doctoral dissertation presented to the Athanaeum of St. Apollinaris, contends that the lay superiors of his institute and of all exempt lay institutes enjoy jurisdiction.[36] If his thesis is admitted—and his arguments indeed seem irrefutable—the suspension incurred by a clerical member who becomes a fugitive is reserved to the major superior of the institute, not only in the Order of Hospitalers but in all exempt lay institutes.[37]

Local ordinaries cannot by canon 2253, n. 3, absolve from this censure of suspension in the case of exempt clerical religious, for the absolution is reserved to the proper major superior specifically as major superior and not as proper ordinary, and the local ordinary is not the major superior of any religious, since canon 504 requires that the major superiors be professed in the institute. For the same reasons it seems that local ordinaries cannot absolve from this censure in the case of religious of other than exempt clerical institutes. However, because of the doubt caused by the opinion which states that in all but exempt clerical institutes the censure is reserved to

[34] Canon 118. Thus, Schaefer, *De Religiosis,* n. 572; Goyeneche, *loc. cit.;* Vermeersch-Creusen, *Epitome,* III, n. 590; Blat, *De Delictis et Poenis,* n. 712; and also the other authors who do not distinguish in regard to lay institutes but merely state that in lay institutes the suspension is reserved to the local ordinary—Cocchi, *De Delictis et Poenis,* n. 262; Ayrinhac-Lydon, *Penal Legislation,* p. 300; Beste, *Introductio in Codicem,* p. 969.

[35] *Institutiones,* I, p. 865, n. 644, nota 7; IV, p. 631, n. 2191.

[36] "Exercitium Jurisdictionis et Superiores Laici ex Ordine Hospitalario S. Joannis de Deo,"—*CpR,* XIII (1932), 51-61, 106-114, 224-231, 291-302.

[37] Smith, *Penal Law for Religious,* p. 103.

the local ordinary, jurisdiction would be supplied to him according to the norms of canon 209.

Ordinary confessors and the confessors who are authorized by canon 519 for the confession of religious who approach them for the peace of their conscience cannot absolve from this suspension by virtue of canons 518, § 1, and 519, since this censure is reserved in the institute or the society by the common law and not by the institute itself.[38]

Since the fugitive can be absolved from his sin without receiving absolution from the suspension,[39] and, if there is danger of infamy or of scandal, is even excused from observing the censure before a declaratory sentence has been rendered,[40] it may appear that canon 2254 cannot be invoked by the confessor. However, canon 2232, § 1, seems to deal only with the cases in which absolution cannot in any way be obtained. Therefore this does not prevent the use of canon 2254 when the conditions for its use are verified.[41] When the recourse is made the superior must be told of the rectified status of the fugitive; and if this be done by the confessor he must use extra-sacramental knowledge. But of course even the use of sacramental knowledge is not excluded as long as the express permission of the penitent has been obtained for its use.

Ordinarily recourse is not morally impossible for a cleric in major orders, and therefore canon 2254, § 3, cannot be employed. However, in a case which is entirely occult and known only to the fugitive, *e. g.*, when a religious has left unlawfully and returns before nightfall,[42] canon 2254, § 3, can be employed. When the crime is occult and recourse is possible, though the suspension is reserved to the proper major superior, the recourse should nevertheless be made to the Sacred Penitentiary, lest a suspicion be created as to the identity of the person if recourse were made to the proper major superior. The Sacred Penitentiary will provide against the revela-

[38] *Supra*, p. 83.

[39] Canon 2250, § 1.

[40] Canon 2232, § 1.

[41] Moriarty, *The Extraordinary Absolution from Censures*, p. 277.

[42] The penalty is incurred the moment the religious leaves with the intention of deserting the institute temporarily and of returning to it later—*Supra*, p. 100.

tion of the delinquent by the automatic privation of office which he incurred if he held any office, and will also enjoin the punishments to be observed by the absolved religious since there will be none inflicted by his superiors.[43]

With regard to the use of the faculties granted on the occasion of jubilee years it must be noted that the faculties depend on the grant of the pope. The constitutions of the Holy See and the *monita* of the Sacred Penitentiary concerning the jubilee must be consulted. On the occasion of the jubilee years of 1925 and 1933 and of their extension to the world in 1926 and 1934 Pius XI gave the faculty to absolve from censures reserved to the ordinary.[44] This faculty gave confessors no power over the suspension incurred by fugitives, since this suspension is reserved specifically to the proper major superior. However, because of the doubt created by the opinion that in all but exempt clerical institutes the censure is reserved to the local ordinary, it seems that confessors on the occasion of the jubilee confession could have absolved fugitives from lay and non-exempt clerical institutes and societies. The doubt gave rise to grounds for using supplied jurisdiction according to the norm of canon 209. But the *monita* of the Sacred Penitentiary issued on the occasion of the jubilees of 1925 and 1934 seemed to exclude this, since they stated that, if a fugitive incurred excommunication by the constitutions of his institute, such an excommunication could be absolved if he was penitent and returned to his institute as soon as possible; but he was to observe the suspension of canon 2386.[45] On the occasion of the jubilee of 1929 Pius XI gave faculties for all *cases* except the excommunication personally reserved to the pope for the violation of the secrecy of the Holy Office and the excommunications *specialissimo modo* reserved to the Holy See,[46] and made no distinction regarding the ecclesiastical authorities to whom these cases were reserved. Thus it seems that confessors by these faculties

[43] Moriarty, *op. cit.*, pp. 277-279.

[44] *Supra*, pp. 49, 50.

[45] S. Poenit., 31 iul. 1924, § IX—*AAS*, XVI (1924), 337-344; 25 febr. 1933, § IX—*AAS*, XXV (1933), 60-65.

[46] Const. *Auspicantibus Nobis*, 6 ian. 1929—*AAS*, XXI (1929), 5-11.

could have absolved all fugitives from the suspension mentioned in canon 2386.

Two questions remain. There is question of the reservation of the suspension in the case of a fugitive in sacred orders who is dismissed. If the dismissed religious or member of a society whose members live in common without vows is still bound by his vows or promises, the reservation of the suspension for the crime of flight is governed by the same laws that obtain for a fugitive who is not dismissed. But the dismissed religious is also under the *ipso facto* incurred suspension of canon 671, n. 1, which suspension is reserved as to its absolution to the Holy See. If the fugitive has been dispensed from his vows or promises in the act of dismissal, then, since the superiors of the institute or society no longer have authority over him, the suspension for the crime of flight is in all cases reserved to the local ordinary, but he also *ipso facto* incurs a suspension according to canon 671, n. 1, which suspension is reserved to the Holy See for its absolution. By analogy of law [47] with canon 1050, which states that when there exist two matrimonial impediments and by indult one can dispense from only one of them the dispensation from both must be sought from the Holy See, it seems that in both of the above cases of dismissed fugitives, since they are under two suspensions one of which is reserved as to its absolution to the Holy See the absolution from both suspensions must be obtained from the Holy See.

Secondly there is the question of the reservation of the suspension for the crime of flight in the case of a one in sacred orders who at the time of his departure had temporary vows or promises which have since expired. In this case also it seems that the suspension for the crime of flight is reserved as to its absolution to the local ordinary, for the superiors of the institute or society no longer have any authority over him. Since he has not lost the diocese which he had before entering the religious life.[48] he is bound to return to his proper diocese and be received by the local ordinary.[49] He has in-

[47] Canon 20.

[48] Canon 585.

[49] Canon 641, § 1.

curred no other suspension than the one for the crime of flight from a religious institute, which suspension is reserved to his local ordinary.

3. The Punishments After Return to the Institute

"*. . . cum autem redierit, puniatur secundum constitutiones, et si constitutiones nihil de hoc caveant, Superior maior pro gravitate culpae poenas infligat.*" If the constitutions enact punishments which are to be inflicted on the returned fugitive, these are to be inflicted by the local or major superior according to the constitutions. If none are stated in the constitutions, then the major superior is to inflict such punishments as are conformed to the gravity of the crime. It is to be noted that the law here differs from the law which treats of the inflicting of punishments on returned apostates. For the latter case it was claimed that the obligation devolves on both the local and major superiors, since canon 2385 makes no distinction.[50] Local ordinaries are not the major superiors of religious, for canon 504 requires that major superiors be professed in the same institute. Therefore, it is not permitted to local ordinaries to inflict punishments for the crime of flight, except according to the norms of canon 2222, § 1, in cases of scandal or special gravity of the transgression even when an exempt religious is concerned, for by the fact being illegitimately outside their religious house the exempt religious does not enjoy the privilege of exemption.[51] Moreover, if the fugitive committed other crimes while he was outside of his institute, then the local ordinary can inflict penalties for these crimes even on an exempt religious if he is not punished by his superiors.[52]

Since the inflicting of penalties after the fugitive returns is committed to the major superior, and since under the term "major superior" are included not only the major superiors of exempt clerical institutes but also those of non-exempt clerical, of lay and even of female institutes and societies, the term "penalties" is not taken in the strict sense of a canonical penalty but in the sense of any

[50] *Supra*, pp. 93, 94.
[51] Canon 616, § 1.
[52] Canon 616, § 2.

punitive measure. Major superiors of exempt clerical institutes, since they enjoy jurisdiction over their subjects,[53] can inflict strict canonical penances, penal remedies and even penalties according to the norms of canon 2222, § 1, if there is scandal or special gravity attached to the transgression.

The punishments are to be inflicted on the returned fugitive according to the norm of the constitutions of the institute or the society, if they make provision for such punishments. In the constitutions of the Friars Minor and of the Calced Carmelites the same punishments are prescribed for fugitives as are enacted for apostates.[54] The Constitutions of the Friars Minor add to the penalties stated in canon 2386 by enacting that a fugitive who is not in sacred orders *ipso facto* incurs a personal interdict which is reserved to the Minister Provincial for its absolution.[55] If the constitutions make no provision for such punishments, then the major superior, and not the local superior, is bound to inflict punishments according to the gravity of the crime. This will be determined by the amount of time that the fugitive was absent and by the circumstances preceding, accompanying and following the fugitive's absence from the religious house.

The obligation of the major superior to inflict the punishments after the fugitive's return is of a mandatory character. Canon 2386 uses preceptive terms.[56] Though superiors are ordinarily bound to inflict these punishments, yet it is committed to their prudence to postpone or abstain from inflicting them or to temper a determined penalty according to the norms of canon 2223, § 3. [57]

It may be added that fugitives are not deprived of the suffrages and privileges of their institute or society except of the privilege of

[53] Canon 501, § 1.

[54] *Supra*, pp. 94, 95.

[55] *The Rule and General Constitutions of the Friars Minor*, n. 125.

[56] Cf. canon 2223, § 3; Blat, *De Delictis et Poenis*, n. 229; Augustine, *A Commentary*, VIII, 473; Woywod, "Apostasy from Religious Life."—*HPR*, XXXIX (1938-1939), 265-274.

[57] These punishments are not necessarily strict canonical penalties, yet it seems that the same norms can be applied.

exemption which exempt religious lose while they remain illegitimately outside of their religious house.[58]

4. Cooperators

Lastly there is the question of cooperators in the crime of flight. All those who concur in the crime of flight in any of the ways defined in canon 2209, §§ 1-3, incur the penalties of canon 2386, of which they are capable, provided that without their cooperation the crime would not have been committed.[59] Thus clerical cooperators who are religious or members of societies whose members live in common without vows incur suspension whose absolution is reserved to their major superior, and also the privation of offices if they held any in their institute or society. Cooperators who are lay religious or lay members of societies whose members live in common without vows incur the privation of offices if they held any in their institute or society. It is to be noted that members of lay societies whose members live in common without vows are here subject to the penalties of canon 2386. By their cooperation they are indirectly subject to the same penalties as the fugitive who is directly subject to them. All the above cooperators, both clerical and lay, are subject to the penalties inflicted on returned fugitives.

5. The Declaratory Sentence

The penalties of the privation of office and of suspension are *latae sententiae* penalties. Hence it is left to the prudence of the ordinary to render a declaratory sentence. But if the common good demands it, then the ordinary, local or proper as the case may be, has an obligation to render a declaratory sentence.[60]

[58] Canon 616, § 1.
[59] Canon 2231; cf. *supra*, p. 96.
[60] Canon 2223, § 4; cf. *supra*, pp. 97-99.

CHAPTER XI

THE OBLIGATIONS OF APOSTATES AND FUGITIVES

Canon 645, § 1. Apostata et fugitivus ab obligatione regulae et votorum minime solvuntur et debent sine mora ad religionem redire.[1]

1. The Obligation of Their Vows, Oath or Promises

By the act of religious profession the religious seals his stability in the religious state with the three public vows of obedience, chastity and poverty, which he is bound by divine[2] and ecclesiastical[3] law to fulfill.[4] Although the religious freely takes upon himself the obligation of the vows, they are of no juridic value unless they are accepted by the legitimate authority.[5] These obligations which the religious has freely taken upon himself can be dispensed only by the pope and by those who are delegated by him,[6] and not by the unlawful and unilateral act of the religious.[7] Likewise, members of societies who live in common without vows seal their stability in their state with an oath or with promises, and cannot abandon the state on their own authority. Therefore apostate and fugitive religious are not freed from the usual three vows of religion,[8] nor from any additional vow or oath which they may have taken in their institute;

[1] Canon 645, § 1. Neither apostate nor fugitive is freed from the obligation of his rule and vows, and must without delay return to his institute. (Authorized English Translation.)

[2] *Summa Theologica,* IIa, IIae, q. 88, a. 12.

[3] Canon 593.

[4] *Supra,* pp. 3, 4.

[5] Canon 572, § 1, n. 6; cf. Suarez, Tr. VII, lib. VII, c. I, n. 1.

[6] *Summa Theologica,* IIa, IIae, q. 88, a. 12; Suarez, Tr. VII, lib. VI, c. XVIII.

[7] Schaefer, *De Religiosis,* n. 568; Toso, *Commentaria Minora,* Lib. II, pars I, tom. III, p. 24.

[8] Canon 645, § 1.

and the members of societies who live in common without vows are under similar circumstances bound by the private vows, the oath or the promises which they have made.[9] Though there is a doubt whether members of lay societies who live in common without vows are subject to the penalties of fugitives,[10] yet there is no doubt that they are subject to the prescriptions of canon 645, § 1.[11]

Canon 1315 states that private vows made before religious profession are suspended while the person who made them remains in religion. Even though apostates and fugitives still belong to the institute, yet they can in some way be said not to remain in religion, and therefore the private vows which they had made before their religious profession revive, since the apostate and fugitive should derive no advantage from his illegitimate departure and in as much as all reason for the continued suspension of these private vows has ceased.[12]

2. The Obligation of the Rules and Constitutions

All religious make profession of the three public vows of obedience, chastity and poverty, but the manner in which they are to be observed is determined by the rules, constitutions and other ordinances of each institute. Wherefore "each and every religious, superiors as well as subjects, is bound not only to faithfully and integrally observe the vows of which he has made profession, but also to order his life according to the rules and constitutions of his institute, and thus tend to the perfection of his state." [13] Therefore, since apostates and fugitives are not freed from the obligation of their religious vows, they are not freed from the obligations of their rule.[14]

In the orders which were founded before the sixteenth century the rule consists of general norms of asceticism and of religious dis-

[9] Canons 681; 645, § 1; Blat, *Ius de Religiosis*, n. 654.

[10] *Supra*, pp. 101, 102.

[11] Canon 681.

[12] Damen, "De Irritatione et Suspensione Votorum Spectato Jure Naturali atque Ecclesiastico Antiquo et Novo,"—*Apollinaris*, III (1930), 274-288.

[13] Canon 593. (Authorized English Translation.)

[14] Canon 645, § 1.

cipline,[15] and the constitutions are the particular determinations made by the chapters and superiors. But in most of the institutes which were founded after that time the constitutions are the principal norms approved by the Holy See, and the rules are the determinations of the constitutions.[16] Some of the modern institutes have no rule. They have only constitutions. The private vows, oath and promises of members of societies who live in common without vows are determined by the rules and constitutions of the society. Therefore, when canon 645, § 1, states that apostates and fugitives are not freed from the obligation of their rule, the term "rule" is to be taken in its widest sense as defined by Schaefer, namely, "all laws and ordinances for the internal government of religious institutes" [or societies].[17] Thus apostates and fugitives are also bound by the customs,[18] statutes, regulations, and other ordinances by whatever title they are called, since it is a general principle that the individual religious cannot dispense himself from these obligations and is not to derive any advantage by his illegitimate departure.[19] Apostate and fugitive religious are moreover subject to the obligations of religious as enacted in canons 592-612, among which are included the obligations of clerics.[20] *Ad instar* apostates and also fugitives from societies who live in common without vows are bound by the clerical obligations and the obligations of religious as stated in canons 595-612.[21] Apostates and fugitives who fail against these obligations are subject to the penalties of canons 2376-2389. Moreover, they are bound to observe the effects of the penalties incurred in canons 2385 and 2386.

[15] The four great rules are the Rule of St. Basil, of St. Augustine, of St. Benedict and of St. Francis.

[16] Schaefer, *De Religiosis,* n. 54; Blat, *Ius de Religiosis,* n. 25; Fanfani, *De Iure Religiosorum,* n. 31; Coronata, *Institutiones,* n. 507.

[17] *Loc. cit.*

[18] Schaefer, *op. cit.*, n. 336; Coronata, *op. cit.*, n. 606.

[19] Reiffenstuel, Lib. III, tit. XXXI, n. 252; Rotarius, *Theologia Moralis Regularium,* Tom. III, lib. II, c. I, punct. IV, n. 2; Passerinus, *De Hominum Statibus,* Q. CLXXXIX, art. VIII, n. 622; Schaefer, *De Religiosis,* n. 568; Coronata, *Institutiones,* n. 643.

[20] Canons 592; 124-142.

[21] Canon 679, § 1.

3. The Obligation to Return

Since apostates and fugitives are not juridically separated from their institute or society, and are consequently bound by their vows, their oath or their promises, and since ordinarily these cannot be observed outside of their institute or society, they are moreover bound to return without delay (*sine mora*) to their institute or society.[22] "Without delay" means as soon as is morally possible. In centralized institutes and societies this return need not be made to the house from which they left. It can be made to any house of the institute or society.[23] But in non-centralized institutes and societies as also in those in which profession is made for a specific house, it seems that they must return to the house which they left.

This obligation to return is surely grave.[24] The authors say that apostates and fugitives are in grave sin until they return to their institute or society.[25] That statement is not entirely accurate. They can certainly free themselves from mortal sin as soon as they make an act of perfect contrition, or as soon as with attrition they go to confession and receive absolution from the censure and from the sin. It would be more accurate to say that they continue in mortal sin until they recede from contumacy. It is true that the purpose of amendment which they must have in making the act of perfect contrition or in going to confession necessarily must include the intention of rectifying their status.[26] But they can do this either by an actual return to their institute or society, or by the serious promise to do so when that becomes morally possible of accomplishment, or by petitioning either for an indult for a temporary absence from the institute or for a dispensation from their vows, their oath, or their promises.[27] In the case of the automatically dismissed the last

[22] Canon 645, § 1.

[23] Pejska, *Jus Canonicum Religiosorum*, p. 188.

[24] Reiffenstuel, Lib. III, tit. XXXI, n. 252; Piatus Montensis, *Praelectiones Juris Regularis*, I, q. 221; Coronata, *Institutiones*, n. 643; Beste, *Introductio in Codicem*, p. 438.

[25] Reiffenstuel, *loc. cit.*; Piatus Montensis, *loc. cit.*; Coronata, *loc. cit.*; Beste, *loc. cit.*; De Meester, *Compendium*, n. 1054.

[26] Moriarty, *The Extraordinary Absolution from Censures*, p. 275.

[27] Berutti, *De Religiosis*, n. 157.

course, namely, a petition for a dispensation from their vows, their oath or their promises, is the only one open to them when superiors refuse to receive them again.[28]

Ordinarily apostates and fugitives will return to their institute and then seek absolution from the censures. Their superiors should obtain the necessary faculties to absolve them if they do not already enjoy these faculties.[29] And then, if the religious have grave reasons to petition for a decree which will permit them temporarily or permanently to live separated from their institute,[30] the application for such a decree should be made through their major superiors.[31] If the apostate or fugitive wishes to be absolved from the censure and desires to petition an indult for his temporary absence or permanent severance from the institute, but does not want to return to his institute for the time which necessarily must lapse before he can obtain it, he should have recourse to his superior for permission to be outside

[28] Superiors are not bound to receive back the automatically dismissed.—P. C. I., 30 iul. 1934—*AAS*, XXVI (1934), 494.

[29] Creusen-Garesché-Ellis, *Religious Men and Women in the Code*, n. 342.

[30] The indult which grants permission to the religious to remain temporarily away from his institute, even though his vows are still binding and there is only a partial relaxation of the bond between him and his institute, is called an *indultum exclaustrationis*. The indult which dispenses the religious from his public religious vows and grants him permission to live permanently away from the institute in view of the severance of all bonds between him and the institute, is called an *indultum saecularizationis* (canon 638-640). These indults can be granted only by the Holy See in the case of religious who belong to institutes of pontifical approval; in the case of religious who belong to institutes of diocesan approval such indults can also be granted by the local ordinary (canon 638). If the religious is in sacred orders and has lost his diocese by perpetual profession (canon 585) it is the present practice of the Holy See to issue simply one indult which grants a temporary absence until the religious finds a benevolent bishop who incardinates him in his diocese, and the indult then automatically becomes an indult the effect of which is that the religious is released from his religious vows and thenceforth is permanently dissociated from all connection with the institute to which he belonged.—Schaefer, *De Religiosis*, nn. 544, 548, 554; Creusen-Garesché-Ellis, *Religious Men and Women in the Code*, n. 336.

[31] *The Constitutions and Rules of the Institute of the Brothers of the Sacred Heart* (Metuchen, N. J., 1928), n. 241, state that a professed brother who voluntarily deserts the institute is himself bound to petition the Sacred Congregation of Religious for a dispensation from his vows.

of his religious house, for the permission to use money and temporal goods, and for a dispensation from the religious observances. Then he can be absolved from the censure and live in the world until the indult arrives.[32] In the case of nuns (*moniales*) this procedure cannot be used.[33] But if the nun is a source of scandal to others some hold that she may be transferred to another convent.[34]

As has been stated, if religious in temporary vows and members of societies who live in common without vows desert their institute or society with the intention of not returning, they are not apostates in the strict sense. They are rather to be called *ad instar* apostates[35] and are not subject to the penalties of the common law for apostasy from a religious institute.[36] Since by their unlawful departure they cannot sever their bond with their institute or society, they too are not freed from their vows, their oath or their promises. Consequently they are bound not only to observe the rule and constitutions but also to return without delay to their institute or society in the same manner as apostates in the strict sense.[37] But in their case these obligations last only as long as the vows, the oath or the promises continue binding, or for such time that a dispensation has not been obtained before their expiration.

[32] Creusen-Garesché-Ellis, *Religious Men and Women in the Code*, n. 342. This is stated in regard to fugitives in *The Constitutions of the Franciscan Friars of the Atonement* (Garrison, N. Y., 1932), n. 354.

[33] Schaaf states that a nun who wishes to leave her cloister for a change of climate is not to leave before an apostolic indult is obtained.—*The Cloister*, The Catholic University of America Canon Law Studies, n. 13 (Cincinnati: St. Anthony Messenger, 1921), p. 140. The present case seems to be an *a pari* situation.

[34] Schaaf, *op. cit.*, p. 138.

[35] *Supra*, pp. 54-57.

[36] *Ibidem*.

[37] Schaefer, *De Religiosis*, n. 568; Woywod, "Apostasy from Religious Life"—*HPR*, XXXIX (1938-1939), 265-274.

CHAPTER XII

THE OBLIGATIONS OF THE SUPERIORS OF APOSTATES AND FUGITIVES

Canon 645, § 2. Superiores debent eos sollicite requirere, et ipsos, si vera poenitentia acti redeant, suscipere; reitum vero monialis apostatae et fugitivae caute curet Ordinarius, et, si agatur de monasterio exempto, etiam Superior regularis.[1]

1. The Obligation to Seek Apostates and Fugitives

Besides the obligation of seeing to the absolution of the censures of their apostate and fugitive subjects [2] and the obligation of inflicting punishments after their return,[3] superiors are bound to seek their apostate and fugitive subjects and receive back the repentant.[4] This obligation arises from the divine law (*iure divino*) by which superiors as shepherds of their flocks are bound to seek those who have strayed and to receive back the repentant.[5] Hence there is no possibility of a custom arising which would abrogate this obligation.[6] Rotarius

[1] Canon 645, § 2. The superiors must seek them with solicitude, and receive them if they return animated by a sincere repentance; but as to apostate and fugitive nuns, the local ordinary shall prudently see to their return, and the regular superior also, in the case of an exempt monastery. (Authorized English Translation.)

[2] *Supra*, p. 116.

[3] Canons 2385, 2386.

[4] Canon 645, § 2.

[5] Conc. Trident., sess. XXIII, *de ref.*, c. 1; St. Alphonsus, *Theologia Moralis*, Lib. IV, n. 82; Rotarius, *Theologia Moralis Regularium*, Tom. I, lib. III, c. I, punct. VI, n. 3; Reiffenstuel, Lib. III, tit. XXXI, n. 259; Ferraris, *Prompta Bibliotheca*, s. v. "Apostasia," n. 58; Piatus Montensis, *Praelectiones Juris Regularis*, I, q. 223; Schaefer, *De Religiosis*, n. 569; Coronata, *Institutiones*, n. 643; Fanfani, *De Iure Religiosorum*, n. 492; Toso, *Commentaria Minora*, Lib. II, pars I, tom. III, n. 241.

[6] Canon 27; cf. Ferraris, *loc. cit.*; Coronata, *loc. cit.*

adds another reason for the obligation of superiors to seek their straying subjects. He says that it belongs to superiors to recover the possessions of the institute and that it is in this capacity that even subjects belong to the institute. But he admits that this cause will rarely urge superiors in conscience.[7] There is no doubt that superiors of societies in which the members live in common without vows are also bound to seek and receive back their subjects who have deserted the society.[8]

As has been stated previous, religious who with the intention of not returning to their first institute in which they still have vows, desert the novitiate of an institute to which they have transferred with an apostolic indult are apostates.[9] The obligation to seek them devolves on the superiors of their first institute.

Before the Code superiors were bound to seek their apostate and fugitive subjects annually.[10] Reiffenstuel stated that superiors did not fulfill their obligation by seeking their straying subjects only once a year, but that they were bound to do so whenever there was any hope of amendment on the part of their subjects.[11] Since no time is stated in the Code it is evident that the obligation of seeking their apostate and fugitive subjects binds superiors whenever, and only as long as, there is some probable hope that the religious or members of a society whose members live in common without vows will amend and return.[12] If there is no hope that they will return, the superiors should warn them that they should seek at least an indult for a temporary absence, or a dispensation from their vows, their oath or their promises, and threaten them with dismissal in the event of non-compliance with the one or the other of these requests.[13]

Since canon 645, § 2, makes no distinction with reference to the

[7] *Theologia Moralis Regularium,* Tom. I, lib. III, c. I, punct. VI, n. 2.

[8] Canons 681, 645.

[9] *Supra,* p. 55.

[10] C. 24, X, *de apostatis et reiterantibus baptisma,* V, 9.

[11] Lib. III, tit. XXXI, n. 259.

[12] Rotarius, *op. cit.,* Tom. I, lib. III, c. I, punct. VI, n. 6; Piatus Montensis, *Praelectiones Juris Regularis,* I, q. 223; Coronata, *Institutiones,* n. 643; Toso, *Commentaria Minora,* Lib. II, pars I, tom. III, n. 241.

[13] Berutti, *De Religiosis,* n. 157.

superior who has the obligation to seek and receive back apostates and fugitives, the obligation devolves not only on the major superiors but also on the local superior of the apostate or fugitive; however, it seems to rest primarily on the immediate major superior who has at his disposal wider facilities for the accomplishment of the task.

The local ordinary shall prudently see to the return of apostate and fugitive nuns (*moniales*), since in this matter all nuns are subject to him.[14] The reason why the local ordinary and the regular superior of the institute of men to whom the nuns are subject are to see to the return of apostate and fugitive nuns inheres in the fact that in view of the law of the papal cloister [15] the superioresses of the nuns may not leave the cloister [16] to seek their straying subjects.[17] The local ordinary on whom this obligation devolves is the ordinary of the place of the house from which the religious left, and not the ordinary of the place of residence of the religious. In this the law differs from canon 2385 in which the excommunication for apostasy from a religious institute in the case of non-exempt clerical religious is reserved to the ordinary of the place where the apostate religious confesses.[18] Even in the case of extern sisters of the monasteries of nuns, when such sisters leave with the intention of not returning, it is the duty of the local ordinary to seek them.[19] In the case of nuns who are subject to the regular superior of an institute of men

[14] Nuns are regulars and if not subject to the regular superior of an institute of men are subject to the local ordinary (canon 615). Nuns subject to the regular superior of an institute of men are also subject to the local ordinary only in the cases stated in the law (canon 500, § 2). Since canon 645, § 1, says that also (*etiam*) the regular superior shall see to the return of apostate and fugitive nuns subject to them, the obligation rests cumulatively on the local ordinary and on the regular superior of the institute of men—Fanfani, *De Iure Religiosorum*, n. 492. This is, therefore, a case stated in the law in which nuns who are subject to a regular superior are subject also to the local ordinary.

[15] Canon 597, § 1.

[16] Canon 601, § 1.

[17] Blat, *Ius de Religiosis*, n. 655; Berutti, *De Religiosis*, n. 157.

[18] Schaefer, *De Religiosis*, n. 569.

[19] "Statuta pro Sororibus externis monasteriorum Monialium cuiuscumque Ordinis," n. 116—*CpR*, XII (1931), 408-425.

the obligation to see to their return devolves cumulatively on the local ordinary and on the regular superior of the institute of men for canon 645, § 2, says that also (*etiam*) the regular superior shall see to their return. The obligation of the local ordinary is not taken away.[20]

The local ordinaries and regular superiors should proceed prudently (*caute*) in seeking apostate and fugitive nuns. This means that they should so act as to obviate all scandal, and to avoid all hardships for either the religious or the institute,[21] and to obstruct all public feeling of misgiving or of wonderment on the part of the laity.[22] As has been stated, in view of the obligation of the cloister, apostate and fugitive nuns who have a grave reason to seek a dispensation from their vows must come back to their monastery, and then petition for a dispensation from their vows, if they want to be absolved from their sin, and in the case of an apostate from the excommunication, before the dispensation arrives.[23]

Though the word *caute* is used in canon 645, § 2, only with reference to local ordinaries and regular superiors in seeing to the return of nuns, yet the same prudence that must actuate them should likewise be exercised by all superiors in seeking their straying subjects. They should use the means that prudence dictates. These means should be such as are the least provocative in starting talk and the best calculated for safeguarding the reputation of the religious and of the institute or society.[24]

The obligations which superiors and local ordinaries have may be fulfilled by them personally or through others.[25] Prudence will dictate which method is to be followed. Sometimes fellow religious

[20] Fanfani, *De Iure Religiosorum*, n. 492.

[21] Schaefer, *De Religiosis*, p. 977, n. 571, nota 153; Blat, *Ius de Religiosis*, n. 652; Biederlack-Führich, *De Religiosis*, n. 169; Beste, *Introductio in Codicem*, p. 438; De Meester, *Compendium*, n. 1054; Cocchi, *De Religiosis et Laicis*, n. 141.

[22] Cocchi, *loc. cit.*

[23] *Supra*, p. 117.

[24] Rotarius, *Theologia Moralis Regularium*, Tom. I, lib. III, c. I, punct. VI, n. 4.

[25] Schaefer, *De Religiosis*, n. 569.

or even relatives and friends will be able to exert more influence on the apostate or fugitive than will superiors.

2. The Obligation to Receive Back Apostates and Fugitives

Superiors are bound not only to seek their errant subjects but also to receive them back. But the obligation to receive them back is dependent on three conditions, namely, that the apostate or fugitive has not been automatically dismissed according to canon 646, § 1; that the religious or the member of a society whose members live in common without vows is animated by sincere repentance in his act of returning; and that the return will not become a scandal or work hardship for the institute or the society.

Superiors are not bound to receive back those who have committed the qualified crimes punished with automatic dismissal according to canon 646, § 1.[26] Superiors are bound to receive back only those apostates and fugitives who are animated by true repentance.[27] This the superiors must do even if the crime of apostasy or flight from the institute has been committed repeatedly.[28] Superiors must receive back even those who want to seek a dispensation from their vows, their oath or their promises after their return. The Benedictine Rule states that apostates and fugitives are to be received back even to a third time.[29] There was a decision of the Sacred Congregation of Bishops and Regulars in the case of a Carthusian which stated that the apostate had to be received back, notwithstanding the clause which provided that he didn't have to be received back after a third time.[30]

Even though the apostate or fugitive in returning is animated by

[26] P. C. I., 30 iul. 1934, ad II—*AAS,* XXVI (1934), 494.

[27] Canon 645, § 2; cf. Passerinus, *De Hominum Statibus,* Q. CLXXXIX, art. VIII, n. 523; Rotarius, *Theologia Moralis Regularium,* Tom. I, lib. III, punct. IV, n. 8; Ferraris, *Prompta Bibliotheca,* s. v. "Apostasia," n. 61; Piatus Montensis, *Praelectiones Juris Regularis,* I, q. 223; Berutti, *De Religiosis,* n. 157; Blat, *Ius de Religiosis,* n. 652; Wernz-Vidal, *Ius Canonicum,* III, n. 433.

[28] Blat, *loc. cit.*

[29] Butler, *Sancti Benedicti Regula Monasteriorum,* c. 29; *MPL,* LXVI, 853.

[30] S. C. Ep. et Reg., 15 dec. 1603—Ferraris, *Prompta Bibliotheca,* s. v. "Apostasia," n. 61.

repentance, his reception is conditioned on the common good of the institute or the society. If superiors think that scandal, undue hardship or grave harm will ensue for the other members of the institute or society, or that regular discipline will suffer by his being received back, they as shepherds of the whole flock and guardians of the common good are not to take back the apostate or fugitive,[31] but are to permit him to remain in the world, to petition for a dispensation from his vows,[32] or they are then to proceed to his dismissal if the scandal arises from the fact that the crime is known to outsiders. The scandal, harm or hardship must be such that it effects the institute or society as a whole. If it can be avoided by transferring the person to another house of the institute or society, this should be done and the superiors cannot refuse to take him back.[33]

3. The Dismissal of Apostates and Fugitives

Relative to the dismissal of those who have deserted their institute or society several distinctions are necessary, dependently upon whether the vows or promises are perpetual or only temporary, and upon whether the person deserted the institute or society with or without the intention of returning.

An apostate in the strict sense is a religious who in perpetual vows deserts his institute with the intention of not returning.[34] Canon 645, § 2, states that superiors and the local ordinary must seek and receive back apostates.. Logically superiors cannot proceed to their dismissal immediately. Moreover, canon 2385 compels the

[31] Rotarius, *Theologia Moralis Regularium,* Tom. I, lib. III, c. I, punct. VI, n. 8; St. Antoninus, *Summae Sacrae Theologiae Iuris Pontificii et Cesarei* (4 tomes, Venetiis, 1571), Pars III, tit. XVI, c. VI, § 1; Berutti, *De Religiosis,* n. 157; Creusen-Garesché-Ellis, *Religious Men and Women in the Code,* n. 342.

[32] *Supra,* pp. 116, 117.

[33] They can proceed to dismissal only if the scandal is known to outsiders. It is then an urgent case of scandal or most grave harm in which the major superior, or even the local superior, can send the religious away according to the norms of canons 653 and 668. The authors sày that this extreme action may not be taken if superiors can provide against the scandal or harm in another way. Cf. Coronata, *Institutiones,* n. 652.,

[34] Canon 644, § 1.

apostate to return, inasmuch as he cannot be absolved from the excommunication until he has rectified, or seriously promises to rectify, his status, and this is ordinarily accomplished by his return to the institute.[35]

The decree *Quum singulae* of 1911 included apostasy from a religious institute among the crimes punished with automatic dismissal.[36] All the preparatory schemata of the Code also included it among the crimes so punished. The Code, though it took away this effect of the crime of apostasy from a religious institute, did not distinguish it from other crimes which are objects of the process of dismissal. If the crime of apostasy were not a possible matter for dismissal, the delinquent who commits this crime could have the assurance of faring better than those who commit other crimes, for they would know that the doors of the institute would never be closed to them, and moreover the institute would have no redress against him by way of dismissing him from the institute.[37]

If the apostate remains contumacious, then the superiors can proceed to dismiss him according to the law.[38] The immediate major superior or his delegate gives a warning[39] with the threat of dismissal.[40] If after three days, computed according to canon 34, § 3, n. 3, the apostate remains contumacious, a second warning is given; and if then he remains contumacious, after at least six days the process for dismissal may be begun.[41] Although but one crime of apostasy was committed, yet the neglect of the warnings assimilates

[35] *Supra*, p. 84.

[36] S. C. de Rel., 16 maii 1911, n. 18, b—*AAS*, III (1911), 235-238; *Fontes*, n. 4409.

[37] Larraona, "Quaestio canonica,"—*CpR*, IV (1923), 174-178.

[38] Larraona, "Quaestio canonica,"—*CpR*, IV (1923), 174-178; Coronata, *Institutiones*, n. 644; Schaefer, *De Religiosis*, p. 977, n. 569, nota 152; Piatus Montensis, *Praelectiones Juris Regularis*, I, p. 214, q. 223, nota 8; Beste, *Introductio in Codicem*, p. 438; Berutti, *De Religiosis*, n. 157; Wernz-Vidal, *Ius Canonicum*, III, n. 433; Goyeneche, *De Religiosis*, n. 102.

[39] Canon 659.

[40] Canon 661, § 3. This holds also in the case of non-exempt clerical and of lay institutes and societies, and even for women religious.—Canons 649; 651, § 1; 681.

[41] Canons 662; 649; 651, § 2.

it to a permanent crime and virtually multiplies its commission.[42] The authors say that superiors should not be rash in proceeding to a dismissal, but should wait for three months,[43] which length of time was required before the apostate was automatically dismissed according to the decree *Quum singulae*.[44]

What is to be done in order to effect the warning of an apostate or fugitive whose place of residence is not known? The Pontifical Commission in answer to this question said that with regard to a fugitive it was sufficiently provided for in the penalties stated for apostates and fugitives.[45] Coronata says that, if either the apostate or the fugitive cannot be located, warnings are *de facto* not required.[46] But Fanfani and Vermeersch-Creusen say that, since the decision was rendered only in regard to fugitives, when there is question of a fugitive that cannot be reached in order to give the warnings the Holy See must be petitioned for a dispensation from the warnings that must be given before the process of dismissal can be begun.[47] If the apostate is cited but does not appear, this does not hinder the process, inasmuch as a physical presence is not required and a juridical presence suffices.[48]

Even after the apostate returns a warning can be given according to the norm of canon 658, § 1,[49] so that, if he repeats the crime within an interval of time that does not morally interrupt the crimes, this warning can be considered one of the two necessary warnings which superiors must administer before they can proceed to dis-

[42] Canon 660; Palombo, *De Dismissione Religiosorum* (Taurini, Romae: Marietti, 1931), n. 35 .

[43] Schaefer, *De Religiosis*, n. 570; Geser, *The Canon Law Governing Communities of Sisters* (St. Louis: Herder, 1938), p. 354; Larraona, "Quaestio Canonica,"—*CpR*, IV (1923), 174-178.

[44] S. C. de Rel., 16 maii 1911, n. 18, b—*AAS*, III (1911), 235-238; *Fontes*, n. 4409.

[45] Not printed in *AAS*. Cf. Schaefer, *De Religiosis*, n. 590, c; Vermeersch-Creusen, *Epitome*, I, n. 757.

[46] *Institutiones*, I, p. 882, n. 655, nota 7.

[47] Fanfani, *De Iure Religiosorum*, n. 509; Vermeersch-Creusen, *Epitome*, I, n. 757.

[48] Schaefer, *De Religiosis*, n. 570; Wernz-Vidal, *Ius Canonicum*, III, n. 433.

[49] Goyeneche, *De Religiosis*, n. 102.

missal. If the religious amends, this crime for which he was warned is not counted among the three which are necessary for dismissal, since there was a moral interruption. It is not determined in the law how much time is to be allowed to an apostate to prove his amendment and to interrupt the crimes, but the authors usually assign three years.[50] The simple interval of time is not an absolute norm, for a religious who gives extraordinary signs of amendment may be considered to have amended after one year by way of analogy with canon 671, n. 7, whereas one who does not diligently avoid the occasions of falling back, or who refuses to repair the scandal by public penance, or who does not show a greater devotion for religious observance may not be considered as having amended even after three years.[51]

The question arises as to what can be done in the case of an apostate who is repentant, but who cannot be received back because of scandal or harm to the institute which scandal cannot be avoided in any way, *e. g.*, by transferring him to another house, and who nevertheless refuses to seek an indult which will permit him to remain temporarily outside of his institute or to seek a dispensation from his vows. He cannot be dismissed, since he is no longer contumacious. Before one can be compelled to live in the world in view of the impending scandal or dire harm to the community, the scandal must be external, *i. e.*, known to outsiders, and the harm to the community must be very grave.[52] The only solution seems to be, to refer the case to the Holy See. Not even women religious can be dismissed even though not crimes but only grave causes are required for their dismissal, for incorrigibility must be present [53] and in the case of one who has repented incorrigibility has ceased.

Another question arises in the case of *ad instar* apostates who are either religious in temporary vows, or who are members of societies whose members live in common without vows, and who deserted the

[50] Coronata, *Institutiones*, n. 655, 1; Creusen-Garesché-Ellis, *Religious Men and Women in the Code*, n. 354; Goyeneche, "Quaestio Canonica,"—*CpR*, V (1924), 21-25.

[51] Schaefer, *De Religiosis*, n. 591.

[52] Canons 653, 668; cf. Coronata, *Institutiones*, n. 652.

[53] Canon 651, § 1.

institute or society with the intention of not returning. As has been stated, they are not apostates in the strict sense [54] and do not incur the penalties enacted in the common law.[55] Those who have vows, or an oath, or promises that are temporary, whether they remain contumacious or whether they return repentant, may be dismissed according to the norms of canon 647, since it is not crimes but only grave causes which are necessary as conditions that will justify their dismissal.[56] Palombo states that when one who is professed with temporary vows commits only one crime the superior is to judge according to the circumstances, namely, by considering what kind of a crime was committed, how much scandal was given, whether the crime was perpetrated with full advertence, what kind of religious life the delinquent has otherwise been living, what consequence the crime will produce and whether there is any hope of amendment. In the main the rule is that "the matter is committed to the judgment and conscience of the superior," who should have at heart the common good of the institute.[57] The same norms of judging circumstances should be used in the case of apostates in the wide sense when only a temporary bond unites them to the institute or society, even though their action is not a crime. Since the deserting of his institute or society by one who is in temporary vows is a cause for dismissal,[58] it is also a cause for refusing to permit the party to renew temporary or to take perpetual vows, or promises, or to renew their oath, that will be binding for a time or perpetually.[59]

In the case of members of societies who live in common without vows who are bound to the society perpetually, but desert the society with the intention of not returning, if their act is punished as a crime in their constitutions, the same methods can be used as are employed with religious who commit the crime of apostasy in the strict sense, for the three crimes which are required as conditions for

[54] *Supra*, pp. 54-57.

[55] *Ibidem*.

[56] Canon 647, § 2, n. 1.

[57] *De Dimissione Religiosorum*, n. 153, 4.

[58] Vermeersch-Creusen, *Epitome*, III, n. 589.

[59] Schaefer, *De Religiosis*, n. 534; Vermeersch-Creusen, *Epitome*, I, n. 749; Palombo, *De Dimissione Religiosorum*, n. 170.

dismissal[60] need not be crimes according to the common law, since it suffices that they be crimes according to the constitutions of the society.[61] But if the constitutions have no such provision, the members of societies of men cannot be dismissed since their act is not a crime.[62] Members of societies of women who live in common without vows who have a perpetual bond to the society and who become apostates in the wide sense can be dismissed if they remain incorrigible since not crimes but only grave external causes are required for their dismissal.[63]

If there is grave external scandal (to outsiders) the superiors can compel the member to leave according to the norm of canon 653 and then begin the process of dismissal. Also if there is scandal or special gravity in the transgression the local ordinary can impose a penalty[64] according to the norms of canon 2222, § 1, since the member has unlawfully left a house of his society.[65] If the member of the society then remains contumacious under the penalty, two warnings can be given; and if he still continues contumacious, the superiors can proceed to dismissal according to the norms of law.

As to fugitive religious who are professed with perpetual vows there is hardly any question of a process of dismissal against them in the capacity of fugitives. Since the authors state that superiors are not to proceed to dismissal until after three months in the case of an apostate[66] it seems that they should wait the same amount of time in the case of a fugitive. After one month, however, superiors will have a presumption of law in their favor that the religious is an apostate[67] and should proceed against him as an apostate.[68] But in the event that it is juridically proved that the religious has not

[60] Canons 681; 649.

[61] Canon 656, n. 1; cf. *e.g., Constitutiones Piae Societatis Missionum* (Pallottine Fathers), n. 205.

[62] Canon 2195, § 1.

[63] Canons 681; 651, § 2.

[64] Canon 2220, § 1.

[65] Canons 679, § 1; 606, § 1.

[66] *Supra*, p. 125.

[67] Canon 644, § 2.

[68] *Supra*, pp. 124-126.

the intention of deserting the institute perpetually he is a fugitive [69] and after three months superiors can proceed to his dismissal, since flight is a crime, and if two warnings have gone unheeded it merits dismissal. Moreover, what has been stated with regard to giving apostates permission to live in the world until they petition for an indult of authorized absence from the institute for a time or for a dispensation from their vows,[70] and what has been stated in regard to repentant apostates whom superiors cannot according to their judgment receive back because of scandal or harm,[71] holds with equal force in regard to fugitives, but the use of these measures should evince greater forbearance and less haste.

As has been stated, the notion of apostasy is applied *ad instar* to members of societies who live in common without vows when a perpetual bond unites them to the society.[72] It seems, therefore, that the presumption of a malicious intention, as stated in canon 644, § 2, will hold also in the case of members of these societies who desert the society. If this presumption is not overthrown the superiors must proceed against him not as a fugitive but as an apostate in the wide sense (*ad instar* apostate).[73] But if this presumption is overthrown they can proceed against him as a fugitive, in the same manner as superiors can proceed against a fugitive religious.

Religious in temporary vows and members of societies whose members live in common without vows who are attached to the society by a temporary bond can be fugitives in the strict sense.[74] They commit the crime of flight. *A fortiori* they can be dismissed for this crime, since it is not only crimes but any grave causes that suffice as conditions for their dismissal.[75] Moreover, superiors can refuse to permit them to renew their temporary or to take their per-

[69] *Supra*, p. 73.

[70] *Supra*, pp. 116, 117.

[71] *Supra*, p. 123.

[72] *Supra*, pp. 54, 55.

[73] *Supra*, pp. 126-128.

[74] *Supra*, pp. 70, 71.

[75] Canons 681; 647, § 2, n. 1.

petual vows, promises or oath.[76] But what has been stated with reference to the consideration of circumstances by superiors when only one crime has been committed by those who are in temporary vows [77] holds with equal force in the case of fugitives who are united to their institute or society with but a temporary bond.

[76] *Supra,* p. 127.

[77] *Ibidem.*

CHAPTER XIII

THE TEMPORAL GOODS, SUPPORT AND BURIAL OF APOSTATES AND FUGITIVES

The Code makes no special provisions with relation to the temporal goods which apostates and fugitives may have had before leaving their institute or society, or the goods that came to them while they were absent, or the dowry of apostate and fugitive women religious, or the debts and expenses contracted while they were absent, or, finally, the burial of apostates and fugitives who die outside of their institute or society. Since apostates and fugitives remain bound by their vows, their oath or their promises, and by their rules and constitutions and the general obligations of religious, in all these matters they are subject to the same laws as are those who do not desert their institute or society. It is to be noted that the law which formerly stated that the property which was acquired by regulars through illicit occupations was to be consigned to the Apostolic Camera [1] must now be considered as abrogated in view of canon 6, n. 6.

1. The Temporal Goods of Apostates and Fugitives

If a religious with simple vows had any property in his own name [2] the status of this property is not changed by his illicit departure. All property coming to the religious while he is unlawfully outside of his institute as an apostate in the strict or wide sense or as a fugitive, by any title on which he can, as a religious with simple

[1] Pius IV, const. *Decens esse,* 5 nov. 1560, § 2—*Bull. Rom. Taur.,* VII, 78, 79; Gregory XIII, const. *Officii nostri,* 21 ian. 1577, § 3—*Bull. Rom. Taur.,* VIII, 162-164; Sixtus V, const. *In conferendis,* 23 ian. 1590, § 17—*Bull. Rom. Taur.,* IX, 165-177.

[2] Religious with simple vows retain the radical ownership of property acquired by them on certain titles, unless a contrary provision is made in the constitutions (canon 580, § 1).

vows acquire and retain its ownership, devolves on the religious. The disposal and administration of property which he had before he left the institute, or which he acquired while he was unlawfully absent, are governed by the same norms as for the disposal and administration of the property which belongs to or devolves on those who do not desert the institute.[3] The property of the members of societies who live in common without vows and any property which was ceded to them while they were unlawfully absent from the society as apostates in the wide sense or as fugitives is governed by the same norms which are invoked in the case of one who has not deserted the society, *i. e.*, they retain the property in their own name.[4] In the event of the death of the apostate or of the fugitive religious or member of a society whose members live in common without vows the property that he had in his own name passes on to his heirs.[5]

All other property which was acquired by a religious with simple vows while he was unlawfully absent from his religious institute either as an apostate in the strict or in the wide sense or as a fugitive, either through his industry or in any other way in which he cannot retain ownership, whether he returned to the institute or died outside of it, devolves on the institute in the same manner as if he had not deserted the institute.[6] All property acquired by members of societies who live in common without vows except that which was acquired in consideration for (*intuitu*) the society devolves on the member [7] and in the event of his death passes on to his heirs.

It can scarcely be imagined that any property will come to an apostate or fugitive in consideration of the institute or the society. But in the event that any such property would come to him it would devolve on the institute or society,[8] whether he had returned to the institute or society or died outside of it.

[3] Canons 569, §§ 1, 2; 580, § 3.

[4] Canon 676, § 3.

[5] Coronata, *Institutiones*, n. 644; Schaefer, *De Religiosis*, n. 569.

[6] Canon 580, § 2; St. Alphonsus, *Theologia Moralis*, Lib. IV, n. 80; Schaefer, *loc. cit.*; Cocchi, *De Religiosis et Laicis*, n. 142; Pruemmer, *Manuale Iuris Canonici*, q. 255.

[7] Canon 676, § 3.

[8] Canons 580, § 2; 676, § 3.

All the property whatsoever that comes to a religious in solemn vows during the time of apostasy or flight, whether because of his industry or on any other title whatsoever, devolves on the order or the Holy See, dependently on whether the order is or is not capable of possessing property.[9] This rule obtains whether the religious has returned to his order or whether he died outside of it.[10]

If members of the laity claim the property of apostates and fugitives in the cases when it should devolve on the institute or the society, then in practice it will be necessary to consult the Holy See as to what is to be done.[11]

2. The Support of Apostates and Fugitives

The question arises as to the obligation of the institute or the society to support an apostate or fugitive. By the act of religious profession the religious makes profession of the three vows and also surrenders himself to the institute which accepts his profession.[12] By reason of the acceptance of the vows and the surrender of the religious to the institute it assumes the obligation, and this in justice, to provide for the temporal and spiritual wants of the religious.[13] It seems that this obligation and the consequent right of the religious to such support is of a conditional character, *i. e.*, the support is to be given, and the religious has a right to it, only in the ordinary way. This is to say that the institute must give the religious the necessities of life *in* the institute and according to the rules and constitutions. Now, the supporting of an apostate or fugitive while he is unlawfully outside of the institute is not the ordinary way of giving a religious the necessities of life. Therefore it seems that the institute has no obligation to use this extraordinary way of support, and consequently the apostate or fugitive has no right to it.

[9] Canon 582.

[10] St. Alphonsus, *Theologia Moralis*, Lib. IV, n. 80; Coronata, *Institutiones*, n. 644; Cocchi, *De Religiosis et Laicis*, n. 142; Schaefer, *De Religiosis*, n. 569; Pruemmer, *Manuale Iuris Canonici*, q. 255.

[11] Pruemmer, *loc. cit.*

[12] Frey, *The Act of Religious Profession*, p. 4; Papi, *Religious in Church Law*, p. 268.

[13] Frey, *op. cit.*, p. 7; Papi, *op. cit.*, pp. 268, 269.

Canon 671, n. 5, states that a dismissed religious who is a cleric in sacred orders must be given a charitable subsidy if he cannot provide for himself. Dismissed women religious are likewise to receive for a time a charitable subsidy if they cannot provide for themselves.[14] Natural equity demands that it be given for a time also to dismissed men religious who are not clerics in sacred orders if they cannot provide for themselves.[15] It may seem that support should in charity be given to apostates and fugitives who are not yet dismissed; but the canons cited above state that this subsidy is to be given to dismissed religious if they cannot provide for themselves, and apostates and fugitives presumably have a way of providing for themselves, namely, by returning to their institute without delay, as they are bound to do.[16] Therefore it must be concluded that the institute is not bound to give a charitable subsidy to apostates or fugitives. However, if in practice the giving of support will induce the religious to return to his institute, the support should be given as a means of bringing back the errant religious; but in many cases the giving of support to them will only serve to prolong their absence.

An objection based on the title of ordination might be raised in the case of clerics who are in sacred orders. They are ordained on the title of poverty, the common table, the congregation, or some similar title.[17] By reason of the title of ordination religious, in the same manner as secular clerics in major orders,[18] have a right to receive support from the institute. Meier, when speaking of the removal of negligent pastors, says that by incardination the secular cleric has a right and an obligation to work in the diocese. He seems

[14] Canon 643, § 2.

[15] Coronata, *Institutiones*, n. 642; Jansen, *Ordensrecht* (3. ed., Paderborn: Schöningh, 1931), p. 281.

[16] Canon 645, § 1.

[17] Canon 982. Members of societies who live in common without vows are incardinated in some diocese (canons 678; 111), unless another provision is made by the Holy See.

[18] Meier, *Penal Administrative Procedure Against Negligent Pastors*, The Catholic University of America Canon Law Studies, n. 140 (Washington, D. C.: The Catholic University of America Press, 1941), p. 215.

to insinuate that the title of ordination gives a cleric *the right to work for his support.*[19] In the case of religious the title of ordination gives the religious cleric in sacred orders the right to work in the institute and thus to obtain his support. It seems, then, that religious clerics have no title by reason of ordination to support *outside* of their institute. This argument is strengthened by the fact that canon 671, n. 5, states that dismissed religious who are clerics in sacred orders are to be given a charitable subsidy if they cannot provide for themselves, and does not mention the title of ordination. If the title of ordination existed effectively for the dismissed there would be no need of a charitable subsidy. Moreover, this charitable subsidy is to be given the dismissed cleric only during the three years during which he is to prove his emendation.[20]

The cleric is bound to return immediately if the institute is willing to take him back before the expiration of the three years.[21] Hence the obligation to give this subsidy to a dismissed cleric in sacred orders binds only during the three years during which the dismissed religious is to prove his amendment and only when the institute will not take him back before the expiration of that time. Therefore if the institute will take him back before the expiration of three years he has no right to the charitable subsidy. A *pari* if the institute is willing to take back the apostate or fugitive in sacred orders he has no right to a charitable subsidy.

To sum up the question of support, it may be stated that the institute has no obligation in justice to support an apostate or a fugitive, nor an obligation to give him a charitable subsidy, except when he wants to return but the superiors cannot receive him back because of scandal, harm or hardship, and the apostate or fugitive is forced to live in the world until he obtains a dispensation from his vows.[22]

In the case of apostates and fugitives who are in sacred orders

[19] Meier, *op. cit.*, pp. 222, 223.

[20] Fanfani, *De Iure Religiosorum*, n. 519.

[21] Coronata, *Institutiones*, n. 658.

[22] Piatus Montensis (*Praelectiones Juris Regularis*, I, q. 219, I, 4) and Schaefer (*De Religiosis*, n. 577) state absolutely and without giving any reasons that the institute is not bound to support apostates.

and who are automatically dismissed from the institute because of the qualified crimes mentioned in canon 646, § 1, since they are deprived of the right to wear the ecclesiastical habit[23] they by that deprivation lose any right to charitable subsidy which they might have otherwise had.[24]

The obligation of supporting an apostate or a fugitive who has been dismissed is governed by the laws, already stated, for the support of dismissed religious.[25]

All that has been said with regard to the support of apostate and fugitive religious holds also for religious who are apostates in the wide sense and for apostates in the wide sense and for fugitives from societies whose members live in common without vows.

As to expenses and debts contracted by apostates in the strict or wide sense and by fugitives, the institute or society is not bound to meet them,[26] unless the institute or society derived some benefit by the apostasy or flight of the member, *e.g.*, through money earned by the apostate or fugitive while absent.[27] This obligation to pay expenses and debts if benefit was derived arises from natural equity.[28] The apostate or fugitive is himself responsible for them,[29] and in justice. The institute or the society is responsible for the expenses necessary to seek and bring back the apostate or fugitive, even though it derives no benefit from his return to his religious institute or society.[30]

[23] Canon 670.

[24] Canon 2304, § 2.

[25] Canons 643; 671, n. 5; and the application of canon 643, § 2, by natural equity to men religious not in sacred orders.

[26] Canons 536, § 3; 676, § 2; cf. Schmalzgrueber, Lib. III, tit. XXXI, n. 277, Rotarius, *Theologia Moralis Regularium*, Tom. I, lib. III, c. I, punct. VI, n. 10; Piatus Montensis, *Praelectiones Juris Regularis*, I, q. 219, I, 4; Schaefer, *De Religiosis*, n. 571; Augustine, *A Commentary*, VIII, 471.

[27] Canon 536, § 4; cf. Rotarius, *loc. cit.;* Schmalzgrueber, Lib. III, tit. XXXI, n. 276; Roderici, *Quaestiones Regulares* (Lugduni, 1634), "De Apostatis," p. 95, n. 9.

[28] Schmalzgrueber, *loc. cit.*

[29] Canon 536, § 3.

[30] Rotarius, *loc. cit.*

In connection with the support of apostate and fugitive religious there arises the question of the restoration of the dowry to women religious who have become apostates or fugitives. Canon 551, § 1, states that "if, from whatever cause (*quavis de causa discedenti*), a professed religious with either solemn or simple vows leaves the institute, her dowry must be returned to her intact, but not the interest already derived therefrom." [31]

The principal purpose of the dowry is to provide a means of support for the religious in the institute.[32] This support is provided from the income of the dowry. Since the institute is not bound to support apostates and fugitives,[33] it has no right to the fruits of the dowry for the period of time that the apostate or fugitive is absent. If the fruits of the dowry mature periodically the institute may retain at the next time of maturity a portion of the fruits corresponding to the amount of time the religious spent within the institute since the last day of maturing of the fruits of the dowry.[34] The remainder of the fruits of the dowry maturing during the time of apostasy or of flight must in justice be returned to the religious. In the case of religious in simple vows this income is added to the patrimony of the religious, or it must be disposed of according to the constitutions if the religious cannot acquire property on such a title. In the case of religious in solemn vows this income, since the religious cannot acquire property, belongs to the order or to the Holy See according to canon 582.

Relative to the question of restoring the dowry itself, the authors who treat the question are divided on the nature of the obligation on the part of the institute to restore it to apostates and fugitives. Some say that there is no obligation to restore the dowry to them, since their separation from the institute is only factual and not juridic, and the religious are bound by canon 645, § 1, to return with-

[31] Authorized English Translation.

[32] Kealy, *The Dowry of Women Religious*, The Catholic University of America Canon Law Studies, n. 134 (Washington, D. C.: The Catholic University of America Press, 1941), pp. 1, 29.

[33] *Supra*, p. 135.

[34] Blat, *Ius de Religiosis*, n. 341; Beste, *Introductio in Codicem*, p. 368.

out delay.[35] Others say absolutely that the institute is bound to restore the dowry whether the religious leaves licitly or illicitly.[36] Although they make no explicit mention of apostates and fugitives, their statement surely includes them. Still others prefer to distinguish by saying that the institute is bound to restore the dowry to apostates and fugitives after all the efforts of the superiors to bring them back [37] have proved futile.[38]

Kealy and Larraona state that the obligation to restore the dowry extends to all forms of departure that from their nature are not temporary but permanent, whether they be legitimate or illegitimate.[39] These authors state that the dowry is to be restored to apostates when superiors cannot induce them to come back, but also state that the dowry is not to be restored to fugitives since their temporary absence does not constitute a departure from the institute in the sense of canon 551, § 1.[40] As has been stated, flight is as much a desertion of the institute as apostasy, the only difference being that apostasy is intended to be perpetual and flight only temporary.[41] Secondly, although there is a presumption of law that after a month the absent religious is an apostate,[42] if this presumption is peremptorily overthrown the religious is a fugitive no matter how long he remains outside of his institute.[43] Lastly, the absence or both the apostate and the fugitive *should* be only temporary, since both are bound to return to their institute without delay.[44] Therefore it seems that no distinction should be made between apostates and fugitives.

[35] Schaefer, *De Religiosis*, n. 231; Blat, *Ius de Religiosis*, n. 342; Beste, *Introductio in Codicem*, p. 368; Creusen-Garesché-Ellis, *Religious Men and Women in the Code*, n. 186.

[36] Fanfani, *De Iure Religiosorum*, n. 171; Coronata, *Institutiones*, n. 577, 5; Toso, *Commentaria Minora*, Lib. II, pars II, p. 111, n. 1.

[37] Canon 645, § 2.

[38] Berutti, *De Religiosis*, n. 73; Kealy, *The Dowry of Women Religious*, p. 115; Larraona, "Commentarium Codicis,"—*CpR*, XXI (1940), 147.

[39] Kealy, *op. cit.*, p. 115; Larraona, *loc. cit.*

[40] Kealy, *op. cit.*, p. 112; Larraona, *loc. cit.*

[41] *Supra*, pp. 73, 74.

[42] Canon 644, § 2.

[43] *Supra*, pp. 68, 69, 75.

[44] Canon 645, § 1.

The present writer is of the opinion that *per se* the institute is obliged to return the dowry to apostates and fugitives, since the dowry is intended as a capital sum the income from which is to support the religious in the institute; and this support is not given to them. But because the departure of the apostate or fugitive should be only temporary, and the dowry will suffer no loss of income if it remains among the investments of the institute, inasmuch as it will bring in about the same income as it would if the religious invested it, and because of the grave inconvenience that would be involved in taking this one dowry from the investments of the institute for the time that the apostate or fugitive is absent, it seems that the institute *per accidens* is not obliged to restore the dowry to apostates and fugitives until they have been dismissed.

As Kealy states, because of the division of opinion, a doubt of law must in all probability be admitted as present, and therefore the institute cannot be compelled to restore the dowry.[45] But by way of policy it should do so in order to avoid any self-interest in the condemnation of the apostasy or flight.[46]

Lastly, if apostates and fugitives are dismissed there is no question that the dowry must be restored to them.

3. The Burial of Apostates and Fugitives

There remains only the question of the funeral of a deceased apostate or fugitive. If they have returned to their institute or society there is no doubt that ecclesiastical burial is to be granted according to the norms of law.[47] Likewise, those who die outside their institute or society, if they gave some probable and positive sign of repentance, are not to be refused Christian burial, if no scandal will arise from its grant.[48]

[45] Kealy, *op. cit.*, p. 115.

[46] Kealy, *op. cit.*, p. 115; Beste, *Introduction in Codicem*, p. 368; Creusen-Garesché-Ellis, *Religious Men and Women in the Code*, n. 186.

[47] Canons 514, § 3; 675; 1221; 1224, n. 2; 1230, n. 5.

[48] Kerin, *The Privation of Christian Burial*, The Catholic University of America Canon Law Studies, n. 136 (Washington, D. C.: The Catholic University of America Press, 1941), pp. 150, 151.

Religious or members of societies who live in common without vows, when they have become apostates from the faith, *i. e.*, when they have *completely* abandoned the Christian faith,[49] are automatically dismissed from their institute or society.[50] If their crime is notorious and if they have given no positive and probable sign of repentance, they are to be denied Christian burial.[51] Likewise, all excommunicated persons, hence all apostates from a religious institute in the strict sense, upon whom a declaratory sentence has been passed, if their crime is notorious (and apostasy usually is),[52] and if no sign of repentance has been given, are to be denied Christian burial.[53]

Lastly, public and manifest sinners, if they have given no signs of repentance, are to be denied Christian burial.[54] As Kerin points out, the words "public" and "manifest" are synonymous with the word "notorious."[55] By canon 1240, § 1, n. 6, the Church certainly punishes with privation of Christian burial those who were guilty of a notorious crime and died unrepentant. But it is doubtful if those who were guilty of a notorious sin which was not a crime according to canon 2195 come under this privation. Hence the latter are not to be deprived of Christian burial unless unavoidable scandal would arise. At times all such possible scandal can be obviated by holding the funeral elsewhere.[56] Apostasy in the strict sense and also flight from a religious institute are true crimes; but apostasy in the wide sense, although it is a grave sin, is not a crime, unless it is punished with an ecclesiastical penalty by the constitutions of the religious institute or society.[57] Hence unrepentant notorious apostates in the strict sense and also fugitives, even though no declaratory sentence has been rendered, are to be deprived of Christian burial; but apos-

[49] Cf. canon 1325, § 2.
[50] Canons 646, § 1; 681.
[51] Canon 1240, § 1, n. 1.
[52] *Supra*, p. 97.
[53] Canon 1240, § 1, n. 2.
[54] Canon 1240, § 1, n. 6.
[55] *Op. cit.*, pp. 140-142.
[56] Kerin, *op. cit.*, pp. 222, 223.
[57] *Supra*, pp. 54-57.

tates in the wide sense are not to be deprived of it unless it was punished with an ecclesiastical penalty by the constitutions of the institute or unless penalties had been inflicted according to the norm of canon 2222, § 1. It seems that a fugitive whose temporary vows, oath or promises expired, but who never repented of his crime, is also to be deprived of Christian burial.

In the case of a sudden or accidental death, by a benign interpretation of the law, ecclesiastical authorities should obviate all scandal by permitting only a less solemn funeral.[58] In all cases in which according to the rigor of the law Christian burial should be denied, but graver possible scandal or harm to the institute or society may result from its denial than from its concession, the course to be followed is that in which a lesser danger of scandal will impend. Usually the danger of such scandal can be obviated, if not also entirely nullified, by an announcement of the signs of repentance, by the granting of a less solemn funeral, *e. g.*, a low Mass in place of a high Mass, or by judiciously employed means.[59]

[58] For a fuller treatment of the question of scandal in regard to Christian burial, cf. Kerin, *op. cit.*, pp. 151-159.

[59] Kerin, *op. cit.*, pp. 152, 154, 155.

CONCLUSIONS

FROM the doctrine as contained in this dissertation the following conclusions may be proposed:

1. Up to the time of the Code the chief penalty in the common law for apostasy from a religious institute was the *ferendae sententiae* excommunication enacted by the Council of Chalcedon (451) (p. 9), and no penalty was stated in the common law for the crime of flight from a religious institute. From the time of Boniface VIII (1294-1303) apostates and fugitives who put off their religious habit *ipso facto* incurred excommunication (p. 31). Up to the time of the Code these penalties bound only regulars and the members of the Society of Jesus (pp. 41, 42). During the period between the decree *Quum singulae* (1911) and the Code apostates from all religious institutes were *ipso facto* dismissed if they did not return within three months (pp. 48, 49).

2. Both apostates and fugitives desert their institute or society. The intention with which they leave distinguishes their crimes (pp. 62, 73, 74). Fugitives must intend to be absent for at least three days in order to incur the penalties (pp. 75, 76).

3. Religious with temporary vows and members of societies whose members live in common without vows who desert their institute or society with the intention of not returning to it are not apostates in the strict sense, nor are they fugitives, nor do they incur the penalties enacted for apostates and fugitives (pp. 54-57). Members of lay societies whose members live in common without vows are not subject to the penalties for flight when they leave with the intention of returning to the society (pp. 101, 102).

4. The penalties enacted for apostasy and flight from a religious institute or society are incurred the moment the person leaves with the necessary intention (pp. 61, 72, 78, 100). None of the penalties are *ipso facto* taken away by the return to the institute or society (pp. 79, 82, 88, 91, 92, 102).

5. Local Ordinaries have no jurisdiction over the excommunication or the suspension incurred by exempt religious (pp. 79, 102-109).

6. Ordinaries have an obligation to render a declaratory sentence when the common good demands it (pp. 97-99, 111).

7. The questions of property of apostates and fugitives from religious institutes and societies and of expenses incurred by them while absent are governed by the same laws as apply to those who have not deserted the institute or society (p. 131). There is no obligation to support apostates and fugitives or to give them a charitable subsidy except in the case when they want to return but superiors cannot permit it because of scandal, harm, etc., and they are forced to live in the world until they obtain a dispensation from their bond to the institute or society (pp. 133-136).

8. Apostates in the strict sense and fugitives are to be refused Christian burial unless they gave signs of repentance (pp. 139-141).

BIBLIOGRAPHY

Sources

Acta Apostolicae Sedis, Commentarium Officiale, Romae, 1909—

Bullarium Benedicti XIV, 3 vols. in 4, Prati, 1845-1847.

Bullarium Romanum, 25 vols. in 24, Augustae Taurinorum, 1857-1872.

Canonical Legislation Concerning Religious, Authorized English Translation, Rome: Vatican Printing Office, 1919.

Codicis Iuris Canonici Fontes cura Emi Petri Card. Gasparri editi, 9 vols., Romae [postea Civitate Vaticana]: Typis Polyglottis Vaticanis, 1923-1939 (Vols. VII-IX ed. cura et studio Emi Iustiniani Card. Serédi).

Codex Iuris Canonici Pii X Pontificis Maximi iussu digestus, Benedicti XV auctoritate promulgatus, Romae: Typis Polyglottis Vaticanis, 1917.

Collectanea in usum secretariae Sacrae Congregationis Episcoporum et Regularium, ed. Bizzarri, Romae, 1863.

Constitutiones Fratrum Sacri Ordinis Praedicatorum, Romae, 1933.

Constitutiones Ordinis Fratrum B. V. M. de Monte Carmelo, Civitate Vaticana, 1930.

Constitutiones Ordinis Fratrum Minorum Sancti Francisci Conventualium, Romae, 1932.

Constitutiones Piae Societatis Missionum, Ratisbonae; Pustet, [no date].

Constitutions and Rules of the Institute of the Brothers of the Sacred Heart, Metuchen, N. J., 1928.

Constitutions of the Franciscan Friars of the Atonement, Garrison, N. Y., 1932.

Corpus Iuris Canonici, ed. Lipsiensis secunda, post Aemilii Richter curas . . . instruxit Aemilius Friedberg, 2 vols., Lipsiae, 1879-1881.

Corpus Iuris Civilis, Institutiones, quas recognovit P. Krueger, *Digesta*, quae recognovit T. Mommsen et rectractavit P. Krueger, *Codex Iustinianus*, quem recognovit et retractavit P. Krueger, *Novellae*, quas recognovit R. Schoell et absolvit G. Kroll, 3 vols., Berolini, 1928-1929.

Holstensius, Lucas, *Codex Regularum Monasticarum et Canonicarum collectus olim a S. Benedicto Arianensi*, ed. M. Brockie, 6 tom. in 3 vols., Augustae Vindelicorum, 1759.

Jaffé, Philippus, *Regesta Pontificum Romanorum ab condita ecclesiae ad annum post Christum natum 1198*, 2. ed. correctam et auctam auspiciis G. Wattenbach curaverunt S. Loewenfeld, F. Kaltenbrunner, P. Ewald, 2 tom. in 1, Lipsiae, 1885-1888.

Mansi, Joannes, *Sacrorum Conciliorum Nova et Amplissima Collectio*, 53 vols. in 59, Parisiis, Arnhem, Lipsiae, 1901-1927.

Migne, Jacques P., *Patrologiae Cursus Completus, Series Graeca*, 161 vols., Parisiis, 1856-1866.

———, *Patrologiae Cursus Completus, Series Latina,* 221 vols., Parisiis, 1844-1864.

Monumenta Germaniae Historica, Legum Sectio I, Leges Nationum Germanicarum, Tom. V, ed. E. von Schwind, Hannoverae, 1926.

———, *Legum Sectio II, Capitularia Regum Francorum,* 2 tom. in 5 vols., ed. A. Boretius et V. Krause, Hannoverae, 1883-1897.

———, *Legum Sectio III, Concilia,* 2 tom. and 1 sup., ed. F. Maassen, A. Werminghoff, H. Bastgen, Hannoverae et Lipsiae, 1883-1924.

———, *Epistolae,* Tom. I, II, III, ed. P. Ewald et L. Hartmann, Berolini, 1867-1899.

———, *Leges* (reprint), 5 vols., Lipsiae, 1925.

Regula Primitiva et Constitutiones Fratrum Discalceatorum Ordinis Sanctissimae Trinitatis Redemptionis Captivorum, Isola del Liri: Soc. Tip. A. Macioce & Pisani, 1933.

Rule and General Constitutions of the Friars Minor, The, Paterson, N. J., 1936.

Sacrosancti et Oecumenici Concilii Tridentini Canones et Decreta, Parisiis et Vesontione, 1832.

Sancti Benedicti Regula Monasteriorum, 3. ed., D. Cuthbertus Butler, Friburgi Brisgoviae: Herder, 1935.

Reference Works

Aertnys, Josephus-Damen, Cornelius, *Theologia Moralis,* 13. ed., 2 vols., Taurini, Romae: Marietti, 1939.

Alphonsus de Liguori, St., *Theologia Moralis,* ed. Gaudé, 4 vols., Romae: Typis Polyglottis Vaticanis, 1905-1912.

Antoninus, B., *Summae Sacrae Theologiae, Iuris Pontificii et Cesarei,* 4 tom., Venetiis, 1571.

Ayrinhac, H. A.-Lydon, P. J., *Penal Legislation in the New Code of Canon Law,* New York: Benziger Bros., 1936.

Avanzini, Petrus, *De Constitutione Apostolicae Sedis,* Romae, 1874.

[Bachofen], Charles Augustine, *A Commentary on the New Code of Canon Law,* 8 vols., Vol. III, 4. ed., 1929; Vol. VIII, 2. ed., 1924, St. Louis: Herder.

Benedictus XIV, *De Synodo Dioecesana,* 4 vols., Lovanii, 1763.

Berutti, Christophorus, *Institutiones Iuris Canonici,* 6 vols., Vol. III, *De Religiosis,* Taurini, Romae: Marietti, 1936.

Beste, Udalricus, *Introductio in Codicem,* Collegeville, Minn.: St. John's Abbey Press, 1938.

Biederlack, Josephus-Führich, Maximillianus, *De Religiosis,* Oeniponte: Rauch, 1919.

Blat, Albertus, *Commentarium Textus Codicis Iuris Canonici,* 5 vols. in 6, lib. II, pars II-III, *Ius de Religiosis,* 3. ed., 1938; lib. IV, *De Processibus,* 1927; lib. V, *De Delictis et Poenis,* 1924, Romae: Apud "Angelicum."

Bouix, D., *Tractatus de Jure Regularium,* 2 vols., Parisiis, 1857.

Bouscaren, T. Lincoln, *The Canon Law Digest,* 2 vols. and 2 sups., Milwaukee: Bruce, 1934-1941.

Brancatus, Laurentius, *Epitome Canonum Omnium qui in Conciliis Generalibus, ac Provincialibus, in Decreto Gratiani, in Decretalibus, in Epistolis, et Constitutionibus Romanorum Pontificum usque ad Ssmi. D. N. Alexandri VII annum quartum continentur,* 2. ed., Venetiis, 1673.

Butler, Cuthbert, *Benedictine Monachism,* London, New York: Longmans, Green & Co., 1919.

Cabassutius, Joannes, *Notitia Ecclesiastica Historiarum Conciliorum et Canonum,* Coloniae Agrippinae, 1725.

Cappello, Felix, *Tractatus Canonico-Moralis de Censuris,* 3. ed., Romae: Marietti, 1933.

Castropalao, *Opus Morale,* 2 vols., Venetiis, 1702.

Catholic Encyclopedia, The, 15 vols., index and 2 sups., New York, 1907-1922.

Cerato, Prosdocimus, *Censurae Vignetes Ipso Facto a Codice Iuris Canonici Excerptae,* 2. ed., Patavii: Typis Seminarii, 1921.

Cervia, Augenius, *De Professione Religiosa,* Bologna: Via Bellinzona, 1938.

Chelodi, Joannes, *Ius de Personis,* Tridenti: Libr. Edit. Tridentum, 1922.

Chelodi, Joannes-Dalpiaz, Vigilius, *Ius Poenale et Ordo Procedendi in Iudiciis Criminalibus iuxta Codicem Iuris Canonici,* 4. ed., Tridenti: Ardesi, 1935.

Cipollini, Albertus, *De Censuris Latae Sententiae iuxta Codicem Iuris Canonici,* Taurini: Marietti, 1925.

Cocchi, Guidus, *Commentarium in Codicem Iuris Canonici,* 5 vols. in 8, lib. II, pars II-III, *De Religiosis et Laicis,* 1922; lib. V, *De Delictis et Poenis,* 2. ed., 1928, Taurinorum Augustae: Marietti.

Coronata, Matthaeus Conte a, *Institutiones Iuris Canonici,* 5 vols., Vol. I and II, 2. ed., 1939, Taurini: Marietti, 1933-1939.

Creusen, Joseph-Garesché, Edward-Ellis, Adam, *Religious Men and Women in the Code,* 3. English ed., Milwaukee: Bruce, 1940.

De Meester, A., *Juris Canonici et Juris Canonico-Civilis Compendium,* 3 vols. in 4, Brugis: Desclée, De Brouwer & Si, 1921-1928.

De Nicollis, Laurentius, *Praxis Canonica sive Jus Canonicum casibus practicis explanatum,* Salisburgi, 1729.

Dictionary of Christian Antiquity, 2 vols., London, 1875-1880.

Esswein, Anthony, *The Extrajudicial Coercive Powers of Ecclesiastical Superiors,* The Catholic University of America Canon Law Studies, n. 127, Washington, D. C.: The Catholic University of America Press, 1941.

Fanfani, Ludovicus, *De Iure Religiosorum,* 2. ed., Taurini, Romae: Marietti, 1925.

Feeney, Thomas, *Restitutio in Integrum,* The Catholic University of America Canon Law Studies, n. 129, Washington, D. C.: The Catholic University of America Press, 1941.

Ferraris, Lucius, *Prompta Bibliotheca Canonica, Juridica, Moralis, Theologica, necnon Ascetica, Polemica, Rubristica, Historica,* 8 vols., Parisiis, 1860-1863.

Frey, Wolfgang, ***The Act of Religious Profession,*** The Catholic University of America Canon Law Studies, n. 63, Washington, D. C.: The Catholic University of America, 1931.

Geser, Fintan, ***The Canon Law Governing Communities of Sisters,*** St. Louis: Herder, 1938.

Goyeneche, Servus, ***Iuris Canonici Summa Principia De Religiosis,*** Romae: Tip. Pol. "Cuore di Maria," 1938.

Hefele, Carolus-Leclercq, Henricus, ***Histoire des Conciles,*** 10 vols. in 19, Paris: Letouzey et Ané, 1907-1938.

Heimbucher, Max, ***Die Orden und Kongregationen der Katolischen Kirche,*** 3. ed., 2 vols., Paderborn: Schöningh, 1933-1934.

Hughes, Philip, ***A History of the Church,*** 2 vols., New York: Sheed & Ward, 1934-1935.

Hyland, Francis, ***Excommunication, Its Nature, Historical Development and Effects,*** The Catholic University of America Canon Law Studies, n. 49, Washington, D. C.: The Catholic University of America, 1928.

Jansen, J., ***Ordensrecht,*** 3. ed., Paderborn: Schöningh, 1931.

Kealy, Thomas, ***The Dowry of Women Religious,*** The Catholic University of America Canon Law Studies, n. 134, Washington, D. C.: The Catholic University of America Press, 1941.

Kerin, Charles, ***The Privation of Christian Burial,*** The Catholic University of America Canon Law Studies, n. 136, Washington, D. C.: The Catholic University of America Press, 1941.

Kurth, Godfrey, ***Saint Boniface,*** Translated from the fourth French edition by Rt. Rev. Victor Day with insertions from the Latest Historical Findings by Rev. Francis Betten, S.J., Milwaukee: The Bruce Publishing Co., 1935.

Lehmkuhl, Augustinus, ***Theologia Moralis,*** 10 ed., 2 vols., Friburgi Brisgoviae: Herder, 1902.

Matthaeucci, Augustinus, ***Officialis Curiae Regularis ad optime defendenda suae Religionis jura in Curia examinanda, satis instructus,*** 2 tom. in 1 vol., Romae, 1702, Venetiis, 1703.

McKenna, Stephen, ***Paganism and Pagan Survivals in Spain up to the Fall of the Visigothic Kingdom,*** The Catholic University of America Studies in Mediaeval History, New Series, Vol. I, Washington, D. C.: The Catholic University of America, 1938.

McNeill, John-Gamer, Helena, ***Medieval Handbooks of Penance,*** New York: Columbia University Press, 1938.

Meier, Carl, ***Penal Administrative Process Against Negligent Pastors,*** The Catholic University of America Canon Law Studies, n. 140, Washington, D. C.: The Catholic University of America Press, 1941.

Michiels, Gommarus, ***De Delictis et Poenis,*** Lublin: Catholica Universitas, 1934.

Molitor, R., ***Religiosi Iuris Selecta,*** Ratisbonae: Pustet, 1909.

Montalembert, The Count de, ***The Monks of the West,*** 2 vols., Boston: Noonan, 1872.

Montensis, Piatus, *Praelectiones Iuris Regularis,* 3. ed., 2 vols., Tornaci: Casterman, 1906.

Moriarty, Francis, *The Extraordinary Absolution from Censures,* The Catholic University of America Canon Law Studies, n. 113, Washington, D. C.: The Catholic University of America, 1938.

Müller, Ewald, *Das Konzil v. Vienne,* Münster, 1934.

Noldin, H.-Schmitt, A., *Summa Theologiae Moralis,* 3 vols., Oeniponte, Lipsiae: Rauch, Vol. I., 26. ed., 1939, Vol. II, 25. ed., 1938, Vol. III, 26. ed., 1940.

Orth, Raymond, *The Approbation of Religious Institutes,* The Catholic University of America Canon Law Studies, n. 71, Washington, D. C.: The Catholic University of America, 1931.

Palombo, Josephus, *De Dimissione Religiosorum,* Taurini, Romae: Marietti, 1931.

Papi, Hector, *Religious in Church Law,* New York: Kenedy, 1924.

Parsons, Anscar, *Canonical Elections,* The Catholic University of America Canon Law Studies, n. 118, Washington, D. C.: The Catholic University of America, 1939.

Passerinus, Petrus, *De Hominum Statibus et Officiis Inspectiones Morales,* 3 vols., Lucae, 1732.

Pejska, Josephus, *Jus Canonicum Religiosorum,* 3. ed., Friburgi Brisgoviae: Herder, 1927.

Pennacchi, Josephus, *Commentarium in Constitutionem Apostolicae Sedis,* Romae, 1885.

Pistocchi, Mario, *I Canoni Penali del Codice Ecclesiastico Esposti e Commentali,* Torini, Romae: Marietti, 1925.

Prümmer, Dominicus, *Manuale Iuris Canonici,* 5. ed., Friburgi Brisgoviae: Herder, 1927.

Rainer, Eligius, *Suspension of Clerics,* The Catholic University of America Canon Law Studies, n. 111, Washington, D. C.: The Catholic University of America, 1937.

Raus, Joannes B., *Institutiones Canonicae juxta Novum Codicem Juris,* 2. ed., Lugduni, Parisiis: Vitte, 1931.

Reiffenstuel, Anacletus, *Jus Canonicum Universum,* 5 tom. in 4 vols., Monachij, 1707.

Roberti, Franciscus, *De Delictis et Poenis,* Vol. I, pars I, Romae: Apud Aedes Facultatis Iuridicae ad S. Apollinaris, 1930.

Roderici, Hieronymus, *Quaestiones Regulares,* Lugduni, 1634.

Rotarius, Thomas, *Theologia Moralis Regularium,* 3 tom. in 2 vols., Venetiis, 1735.

Santi, Franciscus, *Praelectiones Juris Canonici,* 4. ed., cura Martini Leitner, 5 vols. in 4, Ratisbonae: Pustet, 1903-1905.

Schaaf, Valentine, *The Cloister,* The Catholic University of America Canon Law Studies, n. 13, Cincinnati: St. Anthony Messenger, 1921.

Schaefer, Timotheus, *De Religiosis,* 3. ed., Romae: Typis Polyglottis Vaticanis, 1940.

Schmalzgrueber, Franciscus, *Ius Canonicum Universum*, 5 tom. in 12 vols., Romae, 1843-1845.

Schroeder, H. J., *Disciplinary Decrees of the General Councils*, St. Louis: Herder, 1937.

Scott, S. P., *The Civil Law*, 17 vols. in 7, Cincinnati: The Central Trust Co., 1932.

Sebastianelli, Gulielmus, *Praelectiones Juris Canonici, De Personis*, 2. ed., Romae: Pustet, 1905.

Smith, Mariner, *The Penal Law for Religious*, The Catholic University of America Canon Law Studies, n. 98, Washington, D. C.: The Catholic University of America, 1935.

Sole, Jacobus, *De Delictis et Poenis*, Romae: Pustet, 1920.

Suarez, Franciscus, *Opera Omnia*, 26 vols., Parisiis, 1856-1861, Vols. XIII-XVI, *De Virtute et Statu Religiosorum.*

Thomas Aquinas, St., *Opera Omnia*, 24 vols. in 15, Parmae, 1852-1869, Vols. III-IV, *Summa Theologica.*

Toso, Albertus, *Ad Codicem Juris Canonici Commentaria Minora*, 5 vols., Romae: *Jus Pontificium*, 1920-1934, lib. II, *De Personis*, pars I, tom. III.

Turner, Sidney, *The Vow of Poverty*, The Catholic University of America Canon Law Studies, n. 54, Washington, D. C.: The Catholic University of America, 1929.

Van Hove, *Commentarium Lovaniense in Codicem Iuris Canonici*, Vol. I, tom. I, *Prolegomena*, Mechliniae, Romae: Dessain, 1928.

Vermeersch, Arthurus, *De Religiosis Institutis et Personis*, 2. ed., 2 vols., Brugis: Beyaert, 1907.

Vermeersch, Arthurus-Creusen, Josephus, *Epitome, Iuris Canonici*, 3. ed., 3 vols., Mechliniae, Romae: Dessain, 1927-1928.

Vromant, A., *De Bonis Ecclesiae Temporalibus ad usum praesertim Missionarum et Religiosorum*, Lovanii: Desbarax, 1927.

Wernz, Franciscus, *Ius Decretalium ad usum Praelectionum in Scholis Textus Iuris Canonici sive Iuris Decretalium*, 6 vols., tom. III, pars II, *Ius Administrationis Ecclesiae Catholicae*, 2. ed., Romae: Ex Typographia Polyglotta S. C. de Prop. Fide, 1908.

Wernz, Franciscus-Vidal, Petrus, *Ius Canonicum ad Codicis norman exactum*, 7 vols. in 8, Romae: Apud Aedes Universitatis Gregorianae, 1923-1938.

Woywod, Stanislaus, *A Practical Commentary on the Code of Canon Law*, 3. ed., 2 vols., New York, Wagner, 1929.

PERIODICALS

American Catholic Quarterly Review, The, 48 vols., Philadelphia, 1876-1923.

Analecta Iuris Pontificii, 28 vols., Romae, 1855-1868, Parisiis, 1869-1891.

Apollinaris, Romae, 1928—

Archiv für katholisches Kirchenrecht, Innsbruck, 1857-1861, Mainz, 1862—

Commentarium pro Religiosis et Missionariis, Romae, 1920—

Homiletic and Pastoral Review, The, New York, 1900—

Jurist, The, Washington, D. C., 1941—

Neues Archiv der Gesellschaft für ältere deutsche Geschischtskunde, Hannover, Leipzig, Berlin, 1876-1935.

Periodica de Re Canonica et Morali utili praesertim Religiosis et Missionariis, Brugis, 1905—

ARTICLES

Albers, Bruno, "Wann sind die Beda-Egbert'schen Bussbücher verfasst worden, und wer ist ihr Verfasser,"—*AKKR,* LXXXI (1901), 393-402.

Canestri, A., "De Extensione Iubilaei ad Universum Orbem,"—*Apollinaris,* VII (1934), 220-237.

Champaux, Timothy, "The Clerical and Lay State Versus the Religious State,"—*The Jurist,* I (1941), 135-138.

Damen, Cornelius, "De Irritatione et Suspensione Votorum spectato Jure Naturale atque Jure Ecclesiastico antiquo et novo,"—*Apollinaris,* III (1930), 274-288.

Gomez, Maurus, "Studia Canonica,"—*CpR,* VIII (1927), 359-374.

Goyeneche, Servus, "De Transitu ad aliam Religionem,"—*CpR,* I (1920), 21-30, 73-77, 107-112, 217-226.

———, "Consultationes,"—*CpR,* VII (1926), 252-254; IX (1928), 427-433; XIV (1933), 257-265; XVII (1936), 343-353.

———, "Quaestio Canonica,"—*CpR,* V (1924), 21-25.

Larraona, Arcadius, "Quaestio Canonica,"—*CpR,* IV (1923), 174-178.

———, "Studia Canonica,"—*CpR,* XII (1931), 60, 61.

———, "Commentarium Codicis,"—*CpR,* II (1921), 134-139, 168-172; IV (1923), 331-335; X (1929), 445.

Ludlow, John, "Desertion of the Clerical Life,"—*Dictionary of Christian Antiquity,* I, 546.

Maroto, Philippus, "Brevis expositio Constitutionis Apostolicae 'Auspicanitbus' quae Iubilaeum Universale extra ordinem at totum annum 1929 indicitur,"—*Apollinaris,* II (1929), 141-202.

———, "Annotationes,"—*CpR,* I (1920), 97-107.

Oesterle, Gerardus, "Casus in Canonem 2385,"—*Apollinaris,* X (1937), 124-132.

Ronayne, Maurice, "The Religious State,"—*The American Catholic Quarterly Review,* IX (1884), 628-649.

Saucedo, Raphael, "Exercitium Jurisdictionis et Superiores Laici ex Ordine Hospitalario S. Joannis de Deo,"—*CpR,* XIII (1932), 51-61, 106-114, 224-231, 291-302.

Schiwietz, Stephan, "Geschichte und Organisation der Pachomianischen Klöster im vierten Jahrhundert,"—*AKKR,* LXXXI (1901), 461-490, 630-649; LXXXII (1902), 217-233, 454-475; LXXXIII (1903), 52-72.

Schwientek, Alexander, "Elementa status religionis in S. Scriptura et in prima traditione ecclesiastico,"—*CpR,* I (1920), 307-315.

Seckel, "Studien zu Benedictus Levita,"—*NA,* XXXI (1905), 59-139; XL (1915), 15-130.

Smith, Isaac, "Monastery,"—*Dictionary of Christian Antiquity,* II, 1219-1229.

Tabera, Arthurus, "De Ordinatione Status Monachalis in Fontibus Iustinianeis," —*CpR,* XIV (1933), 86-95, 199-206.

Van Hove, A., "Apostasy,"—*The Catholic Encyclopedia,* I, 624.

Vermeersch, Arthurus, "Quaeritur quinam sint casus qui, in can. 518 et 519, vocantur 'in religione' reservati?"—*Periodica,* XIX (1923), 112*-114*.

Voltas, Petrus, "Consultationes,"—*CpR,* I (1920), 270-272.

Woywod, Stanislaus, "Apostasy from Religious Life,"—*HPR,* XXXIX (1938-1939), 265-274.

ABBREVIATIONS

AAS—Acta Apostolicae Sedis.
AJP—Analecta Juris Pontificii.
AKKR—Archiv für katholisches Kirchenrecht.
Bull. Rom. Taur.—Bullarium Romanum, Taurinensis editio.
CpR—Commentarium pro Religiosis et Missionariis.
HPR—Homiletic and Pastoral Review.
Fontes—Codicis Iuris Canonici Fontes.
J (K-E-L)—Jaffé, (Kaltenbrunner, Ewald, Loewenfeld).
MGH—Monumenta Germaniae Historica.
MPG—Migne Patrologia, Series Graeca.
MPL—Migne Patrologia, Series Latina.
NA—Neues Archiv der Gesellschaft für ältere deutsche Geschichtskunde.
P. C. I.—Pontificia Commissio ad Codicis Canones authentice interpretandos.
S. C. C.—Sacra Congregatio Concilii.
S. C. de Rel.—Sacra Congregatio de Religiosis.
S. C. Ep. et Reg.—Sacra Congregatio Episcoporum et Regularium.
S. C. Regularium—Sacra Congregatio super consultationibus Regularium (1586-1601).
S. Poenit.—Sacra Poenitentiaria.

ALPHABETICAL INDEX

BIOGRAPHICAL NOTE

Albert Joseph Riesner was born on July 31, 1912, in Baltimore, Maryland. Upon the completion of his primary education at St. James' School of that city he entered the preparatory college of the Redemptorist Fathers, St. Mary's College, North East, Pa., in September, 1926. In 1932 he received the habit of the Congregation of the Most Holy Redeemer and was professed on August 2, 1933. After his course of studies at the Redemptorist House of Studies, Mount St. Alphonsus, Esopus, New York, he was ordained to the priesthood on June 19, 1938, by the Most Reverend Stephen Donahue, Auxiliary Bishop of New York. Returning to Mount St. Alphonsus he completed another year of study, and then was sent by his Superiors in 1939 to the Catholic University of America for the pursuance of further studies in Canon Law. In June, 1940, he received the degree of Baccalaureate in Canon Law, and in June, 1941, the degree of Licentiate in Canon Law.

CANON LAW STUDIES

1. Freriks, Rev. Celestine A., C.PP.S., J.C.D., Religious Congregations in Their External Relations, 121 pp., 1916.
2. Galliher, Rev. Daniel M., O.P., J.C.D., Canonical Elections, 117 pp., 1917.
3. Borkowski, Rev. Aurelius L., O.F.M., J.C.D., De Confraternitatibus Ecclesiasticis, 136 pp., 1918.
4. Castillo, Rev. Cayo, J.C.D., Disertacion Historico-Canonica sobre la Potestad del Cabildo en Sede Vacante o Impedida del Vicario Capitular, 99 pp., 1919 (1918).
5. Kubelbeck, Rev. William J., S.T.B., J.C.D., The Sacred Penitentiaria and Its Relation to Faculties of Ordinaries and Priests, 129 pp., 1918.
6. Petrovits, Rev. Joseph, J.C., S.T.D., J.C.D., The New Church Law on Matrimony, X-461 pp., 1919.
7. Hickey, Rev. John J., S.T.B., J.C.D., Irregularities and Simple Impediments in the New Code of Canon Law, 100 pp., 1920.
8. Klekotka, Rev. Peter J., S.T.B., J.C.D., Diocesan Consultors, 179 pp., 1920.
9. Wanenmacher, Rev. Francis, J.C.D., The Evidence in Ecclesiastical Procedure Affecting the Marriage Bond, 1920 (Printed 1935).
10. Golden, Rev. Henry Francis, J.C.D., Parochial Benefices in the New Code, IV-119 pp., 1921 (Printed 1925).
11. Koudelka, Rev. Charles J., J.C.D., Pastors, Their Rights and Duties According to the New Code of Canon Law, 211 pp., 1921.
12. Melo, Rev. Antonius, O.F.M., J.C.D., De Exemptione Regularium, X-188 pp., 1921.
13. Schaaf, Rev. Valentine Theodore, O.F.M., S.T.B., J.C.D., The Cloister, X-180 pp., 1921.
14. Burke, Rev. Thomas Joseph, S.T.D., J.C.D., Competence in Ecclesiastical Tribunals, IV-117 pp., 1922.
15. Leech, Rev. George Leo, J.C.D., A Comparative Study of the Constitution "Apostolicae Sedis" and the "Codex Juris Canonici," 179 pp., 1922.
16. Motry, Rev. Hubert Louis, S.T.D., J.C.D., Diocesan Faculties According to the Code of Canon Law, II-167 pp., 1922.
17. Murphy, Rev. George Lawrence, J.C.D., Delinquencies and Penalties in the Administration and the Reception of the Sacraments, IV-121 pp., 1923.
18. O'Reilly, Rev. John Anthony, S.T.B., J.C.D., Ecclesiastical Sepulture in the New Code of Canon Law, II-129 pp., 1923.
19. Michalicka, Rev. Wenceslas Cyrill, O.S.B., J.C.D., Judicial Procedure in Dismissal of Clerical Exempt Religious, 107 pp., 1923.

20. DARGIN, REV. EDWARD VINCENT, S.T.B., J.C.D., Reserved Cases According to the Code of Canon Law, IV-103 pp., 1924.

21. GODFREY, REV. JOHN A., S.T.B., J.C.D., The Right of Patronage According to the Code of Canon Law, 153 pp., 1924.

22. HAGEDORN, REV. FRANCIS EDWARD, J.C.D., General Legislation on Indulgences, II-154 pp., 1924.

23. KING, REV. JAMES IGNATIUS, J.C.D., The Administration of the Sacraments to Dying Non-Catholics, V-141 pp., 1924.

24. WINSLOW, REV. FRANCIS JOSEPH, O.F.M., J.C.D., Vicars and Prefects Apostolic, IV-149 pp., 1924.

25. CORREA, REV. JOSE SERVELION, S.T.L., J.C.D., La Potestad Legislativa de la Iglesia Catolica, IV-127 pp., 1925.

26. DUGAN, REV. HENRY FRANCIS, A.M., J.C.D., The Judiciary Department of the Diocesan Curia, 87 pp., 1925.

27. KELLER, REV. CHARLES FREDERICK, S.T.B., J.C.D., Mass Stipends, 167 pp., 1925.

28. PASCHANG, REV. JOHN LINUS, J.C.D., The Sacramentals According to the Code of Canon Law, 129 pp., 1925.

29. PIONTEK, REV. CYRILLUS, O.F.M., S.T.B., J.C.D., De Indulto Exclaustrationis necnon Saecularizationis, XIII-289 pp., 1925.

30. KEARNEY, REV. RICHARD JOSEPH, S.T.B., J.C.D., Sponsors at Baptism According to the Code of Canon Law, IV-127 pp., 1925.

31. BARTLETT, REV. CHESTER JOSEPH, A.M., LL.B., J.C.D., The Tenure of Parochial Property in the United States of America, V-108 pp., 1926.

32. KILKER, REV. ADRIAN JEROME, J.C.D., Extreme Unction, V-425 pp., 1926.

33. MCCORMICK, REV. ROBERT EMMETT, J.C.D., Confessors of Religious, VIII-266 pp., 1926.

34. MILLER, REV. NEWTON THOMAS, J.C.D., Founded Masses According to the Code of Canon Law, VII-93 pp., 1926.

35. ROELKER, REV. EDWARD G., S.T.D., J.C.D., Principles of Privilege According to the Code of Canon Law, XI-166 pp., 1926.

36. BAKALARCZYK, REV. RICHARDUS, M.I.C., J.U.D., De Novitiatu, VIII-208 pp., 1927.

37. PIZZUTI, REV. LAWRENCE, O.F.M., J.U.L., De Parochis Religiosis, 1927. (Not Printed.)

38. BLILEY, REV. NICHOLAS MARTIN, O.S.B., J.C.D., Altars According to the Code of Canon Law, XIX-132 pp., 1927.

39. BROWN, MR. BRENDAN FRANCIS, A.B., LL.M., J.U.D., The Canonical Juristic Personality with Special Reference to its Status in the United States of America, V-212 pp., 1927.

40. CAVANAUGH, REV. WILLIAM THOMAS, C.P., J.U.D., The Reservation of the Blessed Sacrament, VIII-101 pp., 1927.

41. DOHENY, REV. WILLIAM J., C.S.C., A.B., J.U.D., Church Property: Modes of Acquisition, X-118 pp., 1927.

42. Feldhaus, Rev. Aloysius H., C.PP.S., J.C.D., Oratories, IX-141 pp., 1927.
43. Kelly, Rev. James Patrick, A.B., J.C.D., The Jurisdiction of the Simple Confessor, X-208 pp., 1927.
44. Neuberger, Rev. Nicholas J., J.C.D., Canon 6 or the Relation of the Codex Juris Canonici to the Preceding Legislation, V-95 pp., 1927.
45. O'Keefe, Rev. Gerald Michael, J.C.D., Matrimonial Dispensations, Powers of Bishops, Priests, and Confessors, VIII-232 pp., 1927.
46. Quigley, Rev. Joseph A. M., A.B., J.C.D., Condemned Societies, 139 pp., 1927.
47. Zaplotnik, Rev. Johannes Leo, J.C.D., De Vicariis Foraneis, X-142 pp., 1927.
48. Duskie, Rev. John Aloysius, A.B., J.C.D., The Canonical Status of the Orientals in the United States, VIII-196 pp., 1928.
49. Hyland, Rev. Francis Edward, J.C.D., Excommunciation, Its Nature, Historical Development and Effects, VIII-181 pp., 1928.
50. Reinmann, Rev. Gerald Joseph, O.M.C., J.C.D., The Third Order Secular of Saint Francis, 201 pp., 1928.
51. Schenk, Rev. Francis J., J.C.D., The Matrimonial Impediments of Mixed Religion and Disparity of Cult, XVI-318 pp., 1929.
52. Coady, Rev. John Joseph, S.T.D., J.U.D., A.M., The Appointment of Pastors, VIII-150 pp., 1929.
53. Kay, Rev. Thomas Henry, J.C.D., Competence in Matrimonial Procedure, VIII-164 pp., 1929.
54. Turner, Rev. Sidney Joseph, C.P., J.U.D., The Vow of Poverty, XLIX-217 pp., 1929.
55. Kearney, Rev. Raymond A., A.B., S.T.D., J.C.D., The Principles of Delegation, VII-149 pp., 1929.
56. Conran, Rev. Edward James, A.B., J.C.D., The Interdict, V-163 pp., 1930.
57. O'Neill, Rev. William H., J.C.D., Papal Rescripts of Favor, VII-218 pp., 1930.
58. Bastnagel, Rev. Clement Vincent, J.U.D., The Appointment of Parochial Adjutants and Assistants, XV-257 pp., 1930.
59. Ferry, Rev. William A., A.B., J.C.D., Stole Fees, V-136 pp., 1930.
60. Costello, Rev. John Michael, A.B., J.C.D., Domicile and Quasi-Domicile, VII-201 pp., 1930.
61. Kremer, Rev. Michael Nicholas, A.B., S.T.B., J.C.D., Church Support in the United States, VI-136 pp., 1930.
62. Angulo, Rev. Luis, C.M., J.C.D., Legislation de la Iglesia sobre la intencion en la application de la Santa Misa, VII-104 pp., 1931.
63. Frey, Rev. Wolfgang Norbert, O.S.B., A.B., J.C.D., The Act of Religious Profession, VIII-174 pp., 1931.
64. Roberts, Rev. James Brendan, A.B., J.C.D., The Banns of Marriage, XIV-140 pp., 1931.

65. Ryder, Rev. Raymond Aloysius, A.B., J.C.D., Simony, IX-151 pp., 1931.
66. Campagna, Rev. Angelo, Ph.D., J.U.D., Il Vicario Generale del Vescovo, VII-205 pp., 1931.
67. Cox, Rev. Joseph Godfrey, A.B., J.C.D., The Administration of Seminaries, VI-124 pp., 1931.
68. Gregory, Rev. Donald J., J.U.D., The Pauline Privilege, XV-165 pp., 1931.
69. Donohue, Rev. John F., J.C.D., The Impediment of Crime, VII-110 pp., 1931.
70. Dooley, Rev. Eugene A., O.M.I., J.C.D., Church Law on Sacred Relics, IX-143 pp., 1931.
71. Orth, Rev. Clement Raymond, O.M.C., J.C.D., The Approbation of Religious Institutes, 171 pp., 1931.
72. Pernicone, Rev. Joseph M., A.B., J.C.D., The Ecclesiastical Prohibition of Books, XII-267 pp., 1932.
73. Clinton, Rev. Connell, A.B., J.C.D., The Paschal Precept, IX-108 pp., 1932.
74. Donnelly, Rev. Francis B., A.M., S.T.L., J.C.D., The Diocesan Synod, VIII-125 pp., 1932.
75. Torrente, Rev. Camilo, C.M.F., J.C.D., Las Processiones Sagradas, V-145 pp., 1932.
76. Murphy, Rev. Edwin J., C.PP.S., J.C.D., Suspension Ex Informata Conscientia, XI-122 pp., 1932.
77. MacKenzie, Rev. Eric F., A.M., S.T.L., J.C.D., The Delict of Heresy in its Commission, Penalization, Absolution, VII-124 pp., 1932.
78. Lyons, Rev. Avitus E., S.T.B., J.C.D., The Collegiate Tribunal of First Instance, XI-147 pp., 1932.
79. Connolly, Rev. Thomas A., J.C.D., Appeals, XI-195 pp., 1932.
80. Sangmeister, Rev. Joseph V., A.B., J.C.D., Force and Fear as Precluding Matrimonial Consent, V-211 pp., 1932.
81. Jaeger, Rev. Leo A., A.B., J.C.D., The Administration of Vacant and Quasi-Vacant Episcopal Sees in the United States, IX-229 pp., 1932.
82. Rimlinger, Rev. Herbert T., J.C.D., Error Invalidating Matrimonial Consent, VII-79 pp., 1932.
83. Barrett, Rev. John D. M., S.S., J.C.D., A Comparative Study of the Third Plenary Council of Baltimore and the Code, IX-221 pp., 1932.
84. Carberry, Rev. John J., Ph.D., S.T.D., J.C.D., The Juridical Form of Marriage, X-177 pp., 1934.
85. Dolan, Rev. John L., A.B., J.C.D., The Defensor Vinculi, XII-157 pp., 1934.
86. Hannan, Rev. Jerome D., A.M., S.T.D., LL.B., J.C.D., The Canon Law of Wills, IX-517 pp., 1934.
87. Lemieux, Rev. Delise A., A.M., J.C.D., The Sentence in Ecclesiastical Procedure, IX-131 pp., 1934.

88. O'Rourke, Rev. James J., A.B., J.C.D., Parish Registers, VII-109 pp., 1934.
89. Timlin, Rev. Bartholomew, O.F.M., A.M., J.C.D., Conditional Matrimonial Consent, X-381 pp., 1934.
90. Wahl, Rev. Francis X., A.B., J.C.D., The Matrimonial Impediments of Consanguinity and Affinity, VI-125 pp., 1934.
91. White, Rev. Robert J., A.B., LL.B., S.T.B., J.C.D., Canonical Ante-Nuptial Promises and the Civil Law, VI-152 pp., 1934.
92. Herrera, Rev. Antonio Parra, O.C.D., J.C.D., Legislacion Ecclesiastica sobra el Ayuno y la Abstinencia, XI-191 pp., 1935.
93. Kennedy, Rev. Edwin J., J.C.D., The Special Matrimonial Process in Cases of Evident Nullity, X-165 pp., 1935.
94. Manning, Rev. John J., A.B., J.C.D., Presumption of Law in Matrimonial Procedure, XI-111 pp., 1935.
95. Moeder, Rev. John M., J.C.D., The Proper Bishop for Ordination and Dimissorial Letters, VII-135 pp., 1935.
96. O'Mara, Rev. William A., A.B., J.C.D., Canonical Causes for Matrimonial Dispensations, IX-155 pp., 1935.
97. Reilly, Rev. Peter, J.C.D., Residence of Pastors, IX-81 pp., 1935.
98. Smith, Rev. Mariner T., O.P., S.T.Lr., J.C.D., The Penal Law for Religious, VII-169 pp., 1935.
99. Whalen, Rev. Donald W., A.M., J.C.D., The Value of Testimonial Evidence in Matrimonial Procedure, XIII-297 pp., 1935.
100. Cleary, Rev. Joseph F., J.C.D., Canonical Limitations on the Alienation of Church Property, VIII-141 pp., 1936.
101. Glynn, Rev. John C., J.C.D., The Promoter of Justice, XX-337 pp., 1936.
102. Brennan, Rev. James H., S.S., M.A., S.T.B., J.C.D., The Simple Convalidation of Marriage, VI-135 pp., 1937.
103. Brunini, Rev. Joseph Bernard, J.C.D., The Clerical Obligations of Canons 139 and 142, X-121 pp., 1937.
104. Connor, Rev. Maurice, A.B., J.C.D., The Administrative Removal of Pastors, VIII-159 pp., 1937.
105. Guilfoyle, Rev. Merlin Joseph, J.C.D., Custom, XI-144 pp., 1937.
106. Hughes, Rev. James Austin, A.B., A.M., J.C.D., Witnesses in Criminal Trials of Clerics, IX-140 pp., 1937.
107. Jansen, Rev. Raymond J., A.B., S.T.L., J.C.D., Canonical Provisions for Catechetical Instruction, VII-153 pp., 1937.
108. Kealy, Rev. John James, A.B., J.C.D., The Introductory Libellus in Church Court Procedure, XI-121 pp., 1937.
109. McManus, Rev. James Edward, C.SS.R., J.C.D., The Administration of Temporal Goods in Religious Institutes, XVI-196 pp., 1937.
110. Moriarty, Rev. Eugene James, J.C.D., Oaths in Ecclesiastical Courts, X-115 pp., 1937.

111. Rainer, Rev. Eligius George, C.SS.R., J.C.D., Suspension of Clerics, XVII-249 pp., 1937.

112. Reilly, Rev. Thomas F., C.SS.R., J.C.D., Visitation of Religious, VI-195 pp., 1938.

113. Moriarty, Rev. Francis E., C.SS.R., J.C.D., The Extraordinary Absolution from Censures, XV-334 pp., 1938.

114. Connolly, Rev. Nicholas P., J.C.D., The Canonical Erection of Parishes, X-132 pp., 1938.

115. Donovan, Rev. James Joseph, J.C.D., The Pastor's Obligation in Prenuptial Investigation, XII-322 pp., 1938.

116. Harrigan, Rev. Robert J., M.A., S.T.B., J.C.D., The Radical Sanation of Invalid Marriages, VIII-208 pp., 1938.

117. Boffa, Rev. Conrad Humbert, J.C.D., Canonical Provisions for Catholic Schools, VII-211 pp., 1939.

118. Parsons, Rev. Anscar John, O.M.Cap., J.C.D., Canonical Elections, XII-236 pp., 1939.

119. Reilly, Rev. Edward Michael, A.B., J.C.D., The General Norms of Dispensation, XII-156 pp., 1939.

120. Ryan, Rev. Gerald Aloysius, A.B., J.C.D., Principles of Episcopal Jurisdiction, XII-172 pp., 1939.

121. Burton, Rev. Francis James, C.S.C., A.B., J.C.D., A Commentary on Canon 1125, X-222 pp., 1940.

122. Miaskiewicz, Rev. Francis Sigismund, J.C.D., Supplied Jurisdiction According to Canon 209, XII-340 pp., 1940.

123. Rice, Rev. Patrick William, A.B., J.C.D., Proof of Death in Prenuptial Investigation, VIII-156 pp., 1940.

124. Anglin, Rev. Thomas Francis, M.S., J.C.B., The Eucharistic Fast, VIII-183 pp., 1941.

125. Coleman, Rev. John Jerome, J.C.B., The Minister of Confirmation, VI-153 pp., 1941.

126. Downs, Rev. Joseph Emmanuel, A.B., J.C.B., The Concept of Clerical Immunity, XI-163 pp., 1941.

127. Esswein, Rev. Anthony Albert, J.C.B., Extrajudicial Penal Powers of Ecclesiastical Superiors, X-144 pp., 1941.

128. Farrell, Rev. Benjamin Francis, M.A., S.T.L., J.C.B., The Rights and Duties of the Local Ordinary Regarding Congregations of Women Religious of Pontifical Approval, V-195 pp., 1941.

129. Feeney, Rev. Thomas John, A.B., S.T.L., J.C.B., Restitutio in Integrum, VI-169 pp., 1941.

130. Findlay, Rev. Stephen William, O.S.B., A.B., J.C.B., Canonical Norms Governing the Deposition and Degradation of Clerics, XVII-279 pp., 1941.

131. Goodwine, Rev. John, A.B., S.T.L., J.C.B., The Right of the Church to Acquire Property, VIII-119 pp., 1941.

132. HESTON, REV. EDWARD LOUIS, C.S.C., Ph.D., S.T.D., J.C.B., The Alienation of Church Property in the United States, XII-222 pp., 1941.
133. HOGAN, REV. JAMES JOHN, A.B., S.T.L., J.C.B., Judicial Advocates and Procurators, XIII-200 pp., 1941.
134. KEALY, REV. THOMAS M., A.B., Litt.B., J.C.B., Dowry of Women Religious, IX-152 pp., 1941.
135. KEENE, REV. MICHAEL JAMES, O.S.B., J.C.L., Religious Ordinaries and Canon 198, V-164 pp., 1941.
136. KERIN, REV. CHARLES A., S.S., M.A., S.T.B., J.C.B., The Privation of Christian Burial, XVI-279 pp., 1941.
137. LOUIS, REV. WILLIAM FRANCIS, M.A., J.C.B., Diocesan Archives, X-101 pp., 1941.
138. McDEVITT, REV. GILBERT JOSEPH, A.B., J.C.B., Legitimacy and Legitimation, X-247 pp., 1941.
139. McDONOUGH, REV. THOMAS JOSEPH, A.B., J.C.B., Apostolic Administrators, X-217 pp., 1941.
140. MEIER, REV. CARL ANTHONY, A.B., J.C.B., Penal Administration Procedure Against Negligent Pastors, XI-240 pp., 1941.
141. SCHMIDT, REV. JOHN ROGG, A.B., J.C.B., The Principles of Authentic Interpretation in Canon 17 of the Code of Canon Law, XII-331 pp., 1941.
142. SLAFKOSKY, REV. ANDREW LEONARD, A.B., J.C.B., The Canonical Episcopal Visitation of the Diocese, X-197 pp., 1941.
143. SWOBODA, REV. INNOCENT ROBERT, O.F.M., J.C.B., Ignorance in Relation to the Imputability of Delicts, IX-271 pp., 1941.
144. DUBÉ, REV. ARTHUR JOSEPH, A.B., J.C.B., The General Principles for the Reckoning of Time in Canon Law, VIII-299 pp., 1941.
145. McBRIDE, REV. JAMES T., A.B., J.C.B., Incardination and Excardination of Seculars, XX-585 pp., 1941.
146. KRÓL, REV. JOHN T., J.C.L., The Defendant in Contentious Trials.
147. COMYNS, REV. JOSEPH J., C.SS.R., A.B., Papal and Episcopal Administration of Church Property, XIV-155 pp., 1942.
148. BARRY, REV. GARRETT FRANCIS, O.M.I., J.C.L., Violation of the Cloister.
149. BOLDUC, REV. GATIEN, C.S.V., A.B., S.T.L., J.C.L., Les études dans les religions cléricales.
150. BOYLE, REV. DAVID JOHN, M.A., J.C.L., The Juridic Effects of Moral Certitude on Pre-Nuptial Guarantees.
151. CANAVAN, REV. WALTER JOSEPH, M.A., LITT.D., J.C.L., The Profession of Faith.
152. DESROCHERS, REV. BRUNO, A.B., PH.L., S.T.B., J.C.L., Le Premier Concile Plénier de Québec et le Code de Droit Canonique.
153. DILLON, REV. ROBERT EDWARD, A.B., J.C.L., Common Law Marriage.
154. DODWELL, REV. EDWARD JOHN, PH.D., S.T.B., J.C.L., The Time and Place for the Celebration of Marriage.

155. DONNELLAN, REV. THOMAS ANDREW, A.B., J.C.L., The Obligation of the Missa pro Populo.
156. ELTZ, REV. LOUIS ANTHONY, A.B., J.C.L., Cooperators in Crimes According to Canon 2209.
157. GASS, REV. SYLVESTER FRANCIS, M.A., J.C.L., Ecclesiastical Pensions.
158. GUINIVEN, REV. JOHN JOSEPH, C.SS.R., J.C.L., The Precept of Hearing Mass.
159. GULCZYNSKI, REV. JOHN THEOPHILUS, J.C.L., The Desecration and Violation of Churches.
160. HAMMILL, REV. JOHN LEO, M.A., J.C.L., The Obligations of the Traveler According to Canon 14.
161. HAYDT, REV. JOHN JOSEPH, A.B., J.C.L., Reserved Benefices.
162. HUSER, REV. ROGER JOHN, O.F.M., A.B., J.C.L., The Canonical Crime of Abortion.
163. KEARNEY, REV. FRANCIS PATRICK, A.B., S.T.L., J.C.L., The Principles of Canon 1127.
164. LINAHEN, REV. LEO JAMES, S.T.L., J.C.L., De Absolutione Complicis In Peccato Turpi.
165. MCCLOSKEY, REV. JOSEPH ALOYSIUS, A.B., J.C.L., The Subject of Ecclesiastical Law According to Canon 12.
166. O'NEILL, REV. FRANCIS JOSEPH, C.SS.R., J.C.L., The Dismissal of Religious in Temporary Vows.
167. PRINCE, REV. JOHN EDWARD, A.B., S.T.B., J.C.L., The Diocesan Chancellor.
168. RIESNER, REV. ALBERT JOSEPH, C.SS.R., J.C.L., Apostates and Fugitives from Religious Institutes.
169. STENGER, REV. JOSEPH BERNARD, J.C.L., The Mortgaging of Church Property.
170. WALDRON, REV. JOSEPH FRANCIS, A.B., J.C.L., The Minister of Baptism.
171. WILLETT, REV. ROBERT ALBERT, J.C.L., The Probative Value of Documents in Ecclesiastical Trials.
172. WOEBER, REV. EDWARD MARTIN, M.A., J.C.L., The Interpellations.

www.ingramcontent.com/pod-product-compliance
Lightning Source LLC
LaVergne TN
LVHW050229080826
844660LV00012B/501

* 9 7 8 0 8 1 3 2 2 3 5 7 5 *